# African Migration to Thailand

T0299869

This book, based on exploratory ethnographic research, analyzes the experiences of African migrants in Thailand.

Thailand has always been a regional migration hub with Africans being the most recent. Sitting at the intersection of race and migration studies, this book focuses on the challenges Black and labor migrants face trying to integrate into a society that has had very limited contact with and knowledge about Black Africans. Bringing together research from African, Thai, and European scholars, this volume focuses on forced migrants, such as Somali asylum seekers, and labor migrants, largely African men seeking better livelihoods in niche economies such as gem trading, garment wholesale, and football playing and coaching. The book also includes theoretical contributions to the understanding of precarity and human security, the concept of in/visibility to analyze the challenges African migrants face in Thailand as well as the concept of othering to understand discrimination against Africans. The book also analyzes the Thai migration policy context and the challenges facing Thai policy-makers, law enforcement representatives, and the migrants themselves. While not comparative in nature, this volume directly connects with studies of Africans in other parts of Asia, especially China.

Addressing an important gap in migration research, this book will be of interest to researchers across the fields of migration and mobility studies, African Studies, and Asian Studies.

**Elżbieta M. Goździak** is a former visiting professor at the Adam Mickiewicz University in Poznan, Poland, (2018–20) and Research Professor at the Institute for the Study of International Migration (ISIM) at Georgetown University (2002–18) and Editor-in-Chief of *International Migration*. In 2016, she was the George Soros Chair of Public Policy at the Central European University in Budapest.

**Supang Chantavanich** is Professor Emerita in the Faculty of Political Science at Chulalongkorn University. She was the first Chairperson of the Asia-Pacific Migration Research Network (APMRN). Her research covers a wide range of topics, including forced displacement and labor migration.

# Routledge Series on Asian Migration

For more information about this series, please visit: www.routledge.com/Routledge-Series-on-Asian-Migration/book-series/RSAM

# African Migration to Thailand

Race, Mobility, and Integration

**Edited by Elżbieta M. Goździak and Supang Chantavanich**

Routledge
Taylor & Francis Group

LONDON AND NEW YORK

First published 2023
by Routledge
4 Park Square, Milton Park, Abingdon, Oxon OX14 4RN

and by Routledge
605 Third Avenue, New York, NY 10158

*Routledge is an imprint of the Taylor & Francis Group, an informa business*

*British Library Cataloguing-in-Publication Data*
A catalogue record for this book is available from the British Library

*Library of Congress Cataloging-in-Publication Data*
Names: Goździak, Elżbieta M., 1954- editor. | Suphāng Čhanthawānit, editor.
Title: African migration to Thailand: race, mobility, and integration/
edited by Elżbieta M. Goździak and Supang Chantavanich.
Description: New York: Routledge, 2023. | Series: Routledge Series on
Asian Migration | Includes bibliographical references and index. |
Identifiers: LCCN 2022023814 (print) | LCCN 2022023815 (ebook)
Subjects: LCSH: Africans–Migrations. | Africans–Thailand–Social
conditions. | Africans–Cultural assimilation–Thailand. |
Political refugees–Legal status, laws, etc.–Thailand. |
Political refugees–Government policy–Thailand. |
Migrant labor–Employment–Thailand.
Classification: LCC JV8790 .A64 2023 (print) | LCC JV8790 (ebook) |
DDC 304.8/59306–dc23/eng/20220729
LC record available at https://lccn.loc.gov/2022023814
LC ebook record available at https://lccn.loc.gov/2022023815

ISBN: 978-1-032-26108-9 (hbk)
ISBN: 978-1-032-26110-2 (pbk)
ISBN: 978-1-003-28655-4 (ebk)

DOI: 10.4324/9781003286554

Typeset in Times New Roman
by Deanta Global Publishing Services, Chennai, India

# Contents

# Contributors

**Supang Chantavanich** is Professor Emerita in the Faculty of Political Science at Chulalongkorn University, Bangkok, Thailand. She was the first Chairperson of the Asia-Pacific Migration Research Network (APMRN). Her research covers a wide range of topics, including forced displacement and labor migration.

**Elżbieta M. Goździak** is a former visiting professor at the Adam Mickiewicz University in Poznań, Poland, (2018–20) and Research Professor at the Institute for the Study of International Migration (ISIM) at Georgetown University (2002–18), Washington, DC, and Editor-in-Chief of *International Migration*. In 2016, she was the George Soros Chair of Public Policy at the Central European University in Budapest, Hungary.

**Fatma Swaleh Issa** is currently an accountant at a logistics company in Kenya. In 2016–17, she was a master's student at Chulalongkorn University, Bangkok, Thailand. Her research interests include the dynamics of African asylum seekers in Bangkok.

**Waranya Jitpong** is a researcher at the Asian Research Center for Migration at Chulalongkorn University, Bangkok, Thailand. She has an MA in Mental Health from Chulalongkorn University and an MA in Criminology from Mahidol University. Her research focuses on migration and welfare policy, migrant children, and employment of foreign workers in sea fisheries.

**George Kiarie** obtained a scholarship from the Thai government to study International Development at Chulalongkorn University, Bangkok, Thailand. His research interests focus on West Africans in Bangkok, including refugees, asylum seekers, and stateless people.

**Gabriela Romero** has been working on human rights and social and gender inequality. She has an MA in Global Studies from Humboldt University, Berlin, Germany.

**Naruemon Thabchumpon** is Associate Professor of Political Science at Chulalongkorn University, Bangkok, Thailand. She also directs the Asian Research Center for Migration (ARCM) at Chulalongkorn University. Her research interests include African migrants and urban refugees in Bangkok.

**Nithis Thammasaengadipha** is a researcher at the Asian Research Center for Migration (ARCM) at Chulalongkorn University, Bangkok, Thailand. His research focuses on migration and development.

**Anthony Ukam Unor** is currently pursuing a Ph.D. in International Development Studies at Chulalongkorn University, Bangkok, Thailand. His research interests cover international security and migration studies, including African migrants in Thailand.

**Premjai Vungsiriphisal** is Senior Researcher at the Asian Research Center for Migration at Chulalongkorn University, Bangkok, Thailand. Her research agenda includes integration of migrant children. Previously, she worked with non-governmental organizations on women and rural development.

# Preface

Ideas for books do not fall from the sky. This volume also did not materialize out of thin air. It was inspired by the arrival of several Nigerian and Kenyan graduate students at Chulalongkorn University in 2018. Many of these students received scholarships from the Thai government under the *Thai–Africa Partnership for Sustainable Development*, operated by the Thailand International Cooperation Agency (TICA). Several African trainees were also supported to visit Thailand for internships in development, particularly agriculture and husbandry. These initiatives are an outgrowth of the 2013 *Look West Policy*, which marked a new chapter in the diplomatic relationships between Thailand and several African countries.

The Kenyan and Nigerian students told us about other Africans in Bangkok: Somali and Sudanese asylum seekers and entrepreneurs from different African countries. The students also noticed a variety of young African men playing football on campus.

The faculty and researchers at the Asian Research Center for Migration (ARCM) encouraged the African students to create social networks with the African community and start collecting data. We thought that the African students were well positioned to access the African community, gain the migrants' trust, and use the collected data to inform their theses.

It seemed that it would be easiest to approach the Africans playing football on campus or observing Thai students playing friendly football matches. Indeed, the first encounter with the African football players was quite successful. They were eager to chat with a fellow African. However, subsequent attempts to have more formal interviews were not received as enthusiastically. The footballers became suspicious of our student and wondered why he was so interested in them. None of them were professional footballers. They played football in public spaces in the hope of being scouted by football clubs. Professional footballers, whom we met later on, were much more receptive to our research, as were the coaches working with them.

Other groups of African migrants were approached by our students and researchers, including asylum seekers, traders in clothes and precious stones, and church workers. We were also fortunate to work with a Nigerian doctoral student who eagerly agreed to be part of this project. He has been working in Thailand as a teacher for several years and offered great insights and connections to the African community in Bangkok.

The field research, conducted in 2018–2019 and augmented by additional interviews with policy-makers in 2020, was accompanied by intensive deskwork and analysis of Thai immigration policy and existing immigration statistics from 1995 onward.

Despite challenges resulting mainly from the caution that Africans exercise in dealing with Thais, our international team, composed of emerging researchers from Kenya, Nigeria, Colombia, and Thailand, and senior migration scholars from Thailand and the United States, brought this exploratory research to fruition. We hope readers will enjoy the empirical findings presented in this volume as much as we delighted in collecting and analyzing the data and in writing this book. We hope it will spearhead additional research to provide Thai society with in-depth knowledge about Africans trying to make a home in Thailand, and spur policy debates on how to expand admission of Africans to Thailand and facilitate their local integration.

# Acknowledgments

The production of a multiauthor book like this one, *African Migration to Thailand: Race, Mobility, and Integration*, always requires the participation of numerous individuals. We would like to express our appreciation to all of the contributors to this volume, but especially to the African emerging scholars who have pioneered research on African migrants to Thailand, who have made this book a reality. We greatly appreciate their commitment and their generous response to our invitation to participate in this project.

The editors are particularly grateful to Helena Hurd and Rosie Anderson, our editors at Routledge, and their team for support and guidance in bringing this volume to fruition.

We are also greatly indebted to the anonymous reviewers who critically evaluated the book proposal and provided excellent advice to strengthen the volume.

We wish to thank Michael Medley for his skillful copy editing as well as Sonia Paz Canton and Natalia Lopez, student research assistants from Georgetown University, for their expert assistance in preparing the manuscript for publication. Without their help, finalizing this book would have been a much more daunting task.

Elżbieta also wishes to thank the Asian Research Center for Migration (ARCM) and the Visiting Scholar Program at Chulalongkorn University for their generous support of her visiting position in the summer and fall of 2019. Supang expresses her appreciation to Chulalongkorn Association of the ASEAN Studies Center for its support for this book project, representing a new area of scientific inquiry in Thai and African academic writing.

In Thailand, we are indebted to friends in the Ministry of Foreign Affairs, Immigration Bureau, and the National Statistics Office for sharing unpublished materials on Africans in Thailand. We are thankful to civil society organizations working with African asylum seekers who discussed with us issues related to the refugee status determination (RSD) process.

We also wish to thank each other. While this is not our first collaboration, it has certainly been the most ambitious joint project we have undertaken to date.

Finally, we, and the contributors to this book, wish to express our deepest appreciation and sincere admiration for all the African migrants who generously shared their time and experiences with us. Thank you and stay strong.

# 1 Africans in Thailand

*Elżbieta M. Goździak and*
*Supang Chantavanich*

Thailand is known for its tropical beaches, opulent royal palaces, ancient ruins, and ornate Buddhist temples. In Bangkok, the capital, an ultramodern cityscape rises next to quiet canal communities and the iconic temples of Wat Arun, Wat Pho, and the Emerald Buddha Temple. All these wonders, along with delicious food, attract millions of visitors. In 2019, before the COVID pandemic, Thailand welcomed nearly 40 million visitors from abroad. The vast majority of them were tourists on short-term visits.

Thailand is also a regional migration hub within Southeast Asia. The migrant population in the country stood at an estimated 4.9 million in 2019, a substantial increase from 3.7 million in 2014 (Harkins 2019). Migrant workers from neighboring countries of Myanmar, Laos, and Cambodia constitute the lion's share of Thailand's current population of migrants, but migration to Thailand remains quite heterogeneous and includes stateless persons, asylum seekers, urban refugees, professional workers, foreign investors, foreigners married to Thai nationals, students, and retirees.

While many of the labor migrants will return to their countries of origin once their contracts end, an increasing number of foreigners would like to make Thailand their home. Africans, a group of relatively recent newcomers to Thailand, are among those who would welcome an expanded opportunity to open businesses and settle in the country. The Thai government would like to attract more long-stay foreigners as well. However, they have their sights set on high-net-worth individuals, retirees, remote workers, and skilled talent in sectors such as smart electronics and robotics. Unfortunately, most Africans do not fall into these categories.

The majority of Africans living in Thailand are small-scale entrepreneurs trading in inexpensive cloth and clothing as well as gems. Currently, most Somalis residing in Thailand are forced migrants (Abdile 2010), but Somali and Swahili men and women were the first traders who came to Thailand in the 1990s (Lochery 2012). These traders were the precursors of the South–South cloth and clothing trade (Mangieri 2007) and the

DOI: 10.4324/9781003286554-1

'low-end globalization' (Mathews et al. 2017). When trading infrastructures expanded eastward, non-Muslim Kenyans, especially the Kikuyu, came on the heels of the Somali traders looking to source goods in Thailand, India, Indonesia, Hong Kong, and finally China (Lochery 2012). Approximately 700 African gems traders live in Chanthaburi Province. They constitute the largest African community in Thailand. There are also Africans working as teachers in Thailand. Additionally, African men come to Thailand to play football. There are also asylum seekers and refugees among Africans living in Thailand.

## The scale of African migration to Thailand

Exactly how many Africans live in Thailand remains somewhat of a mystery. According to the Thai Immigration Office, a record number of Africans – 236,338 persons – arrived in Thailand in 2019 (Chantavanich & Jitpong, this volume). The vast majority were tourists. According to the Thai Embassy in Pretoria, 96,499 South Africans received tourist visas in 2019. There is no easy way to discern what percentage were White South Africans and what percentage were Black South Africans, but migration scholars in South Africa indicated that most were affluent whites (personal communication, 2020).

The 2020 Population and Housing Census data was not publicly available at the time of this writing. The National Statistics Office (NSO) indicated that COVID disrupted their work. The available data is over ten years old and comes from the 2010 Census. According to the 2010 Census, 8,166 African expatriates lived in Thailand. The vast majority were male: 5,421 men versus 2,097 females. Most lived in municipal areas (7,518 individuals). The data provided by NSO does not indicate which cities have the biggest share of Africans, but anecdotal information suggests that Bangkok is the biggest destination for Africans, at least initially. The Census data does provide limited breakdown by nationality. The largest number or 2,435 individuals were from South Africa. Again, the data does not differentiate between White and Black South Africans. South Africans are followed by Nigerians; 1,556 Nigerians lived in Thailand in 2010. Most were men; there were only 158 females. Nationals of Central African Republic, Guinea, Cameroon, and Sudan were the next largest groups at 470, 421, 359, and 311, respectively. The data shared by the NSO includes close to 3,900 individuals from Africa designated as 'others.' These are countries with fewer than 300 expatriates each.

The 2019 Thailand Migration Report provides a comprehensive profile of migrant workers from Laos, Cambodia, and Myanmar, but there is no information on Africans. African women are mentioned in passing in a section on sex workers and women trafficked for sexual exploitation (Harkins 2019).

The UN Refugee Agency keeps data on the number of African asylum seekers and the number of African urban refugees approved by the United Nations High Commissioner for Refugees (UNHCR). However, this data is not publicly available. According to the Asylum Access Thailand unpublished information, 185 Africans applied for an asylum in Thailand in 2017–2018. The majority of the applicants were from Somalia (134), followed by Ethiopia (23), and Egypt (15). During the same period of time, UNHCR deemed 336 Africans to be *bona fide* refugees. Again, the vast majority were Somalis (223), followed by Congolese (33), Egyptians (16), Ivory Coast (16), Ethiopia (14), and Sudan (13).

The scarcity of reliable statistical data on Africans residing in Thailand is accompanied by limited literature about Africans in Thailand. The few articles published in academic journals are based on very small samples. Examples include papers on African TESOL teachers (Hickey 2018; N=18), football players (Brill & Siriwat 2016; N=50), and Somali traders (Lochery 2012; N=unspecified). Most of the writings about Africans residing in the country come from news articles. These journalistic accounts focus primarily on African visa overstayers caught by immigration authorities and deported or placed in detention centers to await deportation (Colbey 2018); marriage scams between African men and Thai women (Bangkok Post 2018; Morris & Nguyen 2021); and drug smuggling (Malonde 2019). There are virtually no human-interest stories about the challenges Africans living in Thailand face; there are such stories about other groups of migrants (see Phaholtap 2018 and Sutthavong 2015 on Syrians in Bangkok). The exceptions are news stories about children of African fathers and Thai mothers, especially those who became TV stars or entertainers (Khaosod English 2020; Thaitrakulpanich 2020). With this volume we hope to begin to fill the gaps in knowledge about Africans in Thailand. We trust this book will provide ideas for further research, spur innovative methodological approaches, and thoughtful analyses.

## Who is an African?

While the National Statistics Office includes Egyptians and Sudanese in their data on African expats, not everybody who was born in Africa is considered an African. As Jideofor Adibe (2009) reminds us not all citizens of the countries that make up the continent of Africa accept being called 'Africans.' Within Sub-Saharan Africa, some residents of countries such as Somalia, Mauritania, Niger, and Sudan would prefer to be called Arabs, not Africans. Ali Mazrui, an African political scientist, made a distinction between 'Africans of the blood and Africans of the soil.' For him, Africans of the blood are defined in racial and genealogical terms. They are identified with the Black race (race here is understood as a social construct, not a biological distinction) while Africans of the soil are defined in geographical terms (Mazrui 2009).

In this volume, we use the designation 'African' as an *emic* (insider's) category. All the participants in this research self-identified as Africans. They are all Black Africans, mainly but not exclusively, from several Sub-Saharan countries. The asylum seekers interviewed in the course of this research hail from Somalia and Sudan. The vast majority of the clothing traders and cargo entrepreneurs come from Nigeria. The gemstone traders are from Guinea, Mali, Ghana, the Ivory Coast, Senegal, Togo, Sierra Leone, South Africa, Mozambique, and Zambia. The football players are from Angola and Cameroon. The graduate students involved in this research hailed from Kenya and Nigeria.

## The research that informs this book

This book is based on exploratory research. Exploratory research is defined as research used to investigate an issue that is new, a problem which is not clearly defined, a topic on which there is little data (Stebbins 2001). As such, exploratory research does not provide conclusive findings, rather it identifies themes, new areas of inquiry, and research questions for further study. Exploratory research has been widely used in migration studies (Yalaz & Zapata-Barrero 2018), including studies of African migration (Cummings et al. 2021; Nyabvudzi & Chinyamurindi 2019; Hebbani & Preece 2015).

There was no one singular research question that guided all of our research. Rather, each scholar began their field research with a particular group of African migrants in mind or a theme that was of special interest to them. Often times previous connections and easy access to a particular population determined the topical focus of each study. All researchers spearheaded their inquiry with what James Spradley (1979) called a 'grand tour' question, an open-ended question that allowed them to select how they wanted to orient the research topic. Probing questions followed to elicit more specific information, create additional research questions, and identify themes the authors wanted to explore.

The contributors to this volume did not adopt one singular theory either. Rather, they deployed different theoretical frameworks that suited the analysis of the collected data best. As a result, authors explored integration issues within theories of precarity and human security and used the concept of in/visibility to understand the challenges African migrants face in Thailand (Issa); conceptualized precarity not only as an economic issue, but also looked at legal precarity and the survival strategies deployed to ensure both decent livelihoods and legal stability (Kiarie); used the concept of othering to understand discrimination against African entrepreneurs (Unor & Naruemon Thabchumpon); discussed the integration of African footballers on and off the field using social becoming as a collective practice to overcome one's state of what Bloch (1986) calls the state of *not-yet* (Romero & Thammasaengadipha); and framed economic and social integration of African gemstone traders in Chanthaburi as niche economy and niche migration (Vungsiriphisal). Within these diverse research foci and diverse theoretical frameworks, three major themes surfaced: race, mobility, and integration. They appear in the title of this book and crisscross each and every chapter. They are further explored in Chapter 2 (Goździak).

While not comparative in nature, our research directly connects with studies of Africans in other parts of Asia. Studies of African transnational mobility in China (Castillo 2021), Africans in Guangzhou in South China (Mathews et al. 2017), African diaspora in China and the politics of belonging (Lan 2017), circumstantial migration of Gambians to China (Carling & Haugen 2020), and African brokers (Haugen 2018), in particular, have served as an inspiration for this research and analysis.

## A note on the research process

The research team employed a range of qualitative data collection techniques, including participant observation, in-depth semi-structured interviews, and focus group discussions. The vast majority of the interviews and focus group discussions were conducted in person. Interviews with African migrants were conducted in English, on occasion with the help of an interpreter. Interviews with Thai policy-makers, school administrators, teachers, and migrant advocates were conducted in Thai.

Several members of the research team also engaged in participant observation at meetings and workshops set up by legal aid organizations serving African asylum seekers and migrant advocacy agencies. Muslim migrants invited researchers to join them for *iftar*, the fast-breaking meal during the holy month of Ramadhan. Through these home visits, researchers were able to observe daily life of urban refugees and migrants in Bangkok. Using participant observation techniques, researchers were able to understand the studied migrants in a more casual way, without the formality of a structured interview. The combination of informal conversations during participant observation and formal ethnographic interviews provided an opportunity to get a more in-depth insight into their lives.

Whenever possible and with the consent of the study participants, researchers tape-recorded the interviews, but the majority relied on note-taking during and after interviews to remember as many details as possible. Taped-interviews were transcribed and analyzed along with interview notes using a simple content analysis to identify recurring themes.

Careful measures were taken to ensure the study participants' anonymity. This was important to the research team since we witnessed how cautious many of our interlocutors were to not be identified by strangers. The anonymity of the participants was protected by using pseudonyms. Although the interviewed refugees and asylum seekers were quite comfortable naming the neighborhoods they lived in and the streets they walked, we took some precautions and changed many of the details they shared to further anonymize the data.

Much has been written about reflexivity (Berger 2015) and positionality (Bourke 2014) of the researcher/s conducting qualitative studies. After all, research is shaped by both researcher/s and study participant/s (England 1994). In positionality theory, it is acknowledged that because we have multiple overlapping identities, we make meaning from various aspects of those identities (Kezar 2002). The researchers had much in common with the study participants. Several were born, raised, and educated in different African countries. Two of the researchers were migrants themselves: one to Thailand and one to the United States. The research team included both men and women of different ages and different expertise in migration studies. The team included six emerging scholars hailing from Kenya, Nigeria, Colombia, and Thailand. Four senior scholars from Thailand and the United States (via Poland) provided guidance to the younger colleagues and analyzed the data. The team members received training in migration and development, political science, education, sociology, and anthropology.

## The content and structure of the book

We open the book with a Preface that explains how this volume came about. A short introductory chapter presenting the scale and diversity of African newcomers and discussing the research that informs the edited volume follows. In Chapter 2, Elżbieta M. Goździak writes about mobility, race, and integration. She unpacks these three themes to provide a broader context for the empirical findings presented in this volume. In Chapter 3, Supang Chantavanich and Waranya Jitpong discuss Thai visa policies against which migration, both forced and economic, and mobility between Africa and Thailand unfold. The authors analyze visa provisions that facilitate or impede settlement of Africans in Thailand. A brief mapping of the different groups of Africans currently residing in Thailand follows. The chapter ends with policy recommendations aimed at immigration authorities and other branches of the Thai government responsible for foreigners residing in the country. These two chapters serve as a backdrop for the rest of the book.

Fatma Issa (Chapter 4) and George Kiarie (Chapter 5) take a close look at Somalis seeking asylum in Thailand. While both chapters explore the challenges facing Somali asylum seekers, Issa focuses on the struggles of female refugees, while Kiarie presents case studies of two males and one female Somali who left the same part of Somalia fearing for their lives, but chose very distinct paths to come to Thailand. As a result, the protagonists of this chapter became an urban asylum seeker, a student, and a trader, respectively. Issa positions her analysis at the intersection of (in)visibility and human security, especially economic security, while Kiarie places his analysis within the theoretical concept of precarity.

The three chapters that follow explore issues facing African migrants operating in three different niche economies. In Chapter 6, Anthony Unor and Naruemon Thabchumpon look at Nigerian cloth and clothing traders and analyze how encounters with Nigerian migrants contribute to the ways representatives of the Thai government, media, and the wider society construe cultural representations of the African 'Other.' They explore how these representations affect Thais' attitudes towards Black Africans living in Thailand. They situate their analysis at the intersection of race, illegality, and gender (in this case, masculinity). In Chapter 7, Premjai Vungsiriphisal unpacks integration challenges of African gemstone traders in Chanthaburi. In Chapter 8, Gabriela Romero and Nithis Thammasaengadipha discuss another form of niche migration, namely mobility of African footballers. In the final chapter, Elżbieta M. Goździak and Supang Chantavanich identify areas for further research, including applied studies, that would contribute to sound policymaking and facilitate better understanding of African migrants and improve relations between African newcomers and members of the host society.

# References

Abdile, Mahdi. (2010). 'Diasporas and Their Role in the Homeland Conflicts and Peacebuilding: The Case of Somali Diaspora,' *Working Paper 7, Diaspeace Project*. Jyväskylä: University of Jyväskylä.

Adibe, Jideofor (Ed.). (2009). *Who is an African? Identity, Citizenship and the Making of an Africa-Nation*. London: Adonis & Abbey Publishers.

Bangkok Post. (2018). '5 Nigerians, 12 Thais Held in Romance Scams,' *Bangkok Post*, 15 September. Available at: https://www.bangkokpost.com/thailand/general/1540570/5-nigerians-12-thais-held-in-romance-scams

Berger, Roni. (2015). 'Now I See it, Now I Don't: Researcher's Position and Reflexivity in Qualitative Research,' *Qualitative Research*, 15 (2), pp. 219–34. doi:10.1177/1468794112468475

Bloch, Ernst. (1986). *The Principle of Hope*. Cambridge: MIT Press.

Bourke, Brian. (2014). 'Positionality: Reflecting on the Research Process,' *The Qualitative Report*, 19 (33), pp. 1–9.

Brill, Carolina & Siriwat, Chuenchanok Nin. (2016). 'Chao Amigos! Hello Thailand: Football, Migration and Sustainability in Thailand,' *Soccer and Society*, 17 (5), pp. 680–91.

Carling, Jørgen & Heidi Østbø Haugen. (2020). 'Circumstantial Migration: How Gambian Journeys to China Enrich Migration Theory,' *Journal of Ethnic and Migration Studies*, 47 (12), pp. 2778–95. doi: 10.1080/1369183X.2020.1739385

Castillo, Roberto. (2021). *African Transnational Mobility in China. Africans on The Move*. London: Routledge Press.

Colbey, Adele. (2018). 'Arbitrary Arrests Make Life in Bangkok Hell for African Migrants,' *Prachatai English*, 20 June. Available at: https://prachatai.com/english/node/7773

Cumming, Craig, Butt, Julia, Hersi, Abdi, Tohow, Ahmed, & Young, Jesse. (2021). 'Khat Use and Perceived Health Problems Among African Migrants in Australia: An Exploratory Study,' *Eastern Mediterranean Health Journal*, 27 (5), pp. 491–500.

England, K.V.L. (1994). 'Getting Personal: Reflexivity, Positionality, and Feminist Research,' *The Professional Geographer*, 46 (1), pp. 80–89.

Harkins, Benjamin. (2019). 'Thailand Migration Report 2019,' *United Nations Thematic Working Group on Migration in Thailand*. Available at: https://thailand.iom.int/thailand-migration-report-2019-0

Haugen, Østbø Heidi. (2018). 'From Pioneers to Professionals: African Brokers in a Maturing Chinese Marketplace,' *African Studies Quarterly*, 17 (4), pp. 45–62.

Hebbani, Aparna & Preece, Megan. (2015). 'Spoken English Does Matter: Findings from an Exploratory Study to Identify Predictors of Employment among African Refugees in Brisbane,' *The Australasian Review of African Studies*, 36 (2), pp. 110–29. Available at: https://search.informit.org/doi/10.3316/informit.640661581186422

Hickey, Maureen. (2018). 'Thailand's "English Fever," Migrant Teachers and Cosmopolitan Aspirations in an Interconnected Asia,' *Discourse: Studies in the Cultural Politics of Education*, 39 (5), pp. 738–51.

Kezar, Adrianna. (2002). 'Reconstructing Static Images of Leadership: An Application of Positionality Theory,' *Journal of Leadership Studies*, 8 (3), pp. 94–109.

Khaosod English. (2020). 'What it's like to be Half Black, Half Thai: Morris K's Story,' Available at: https://www.khaosodenglish.com/life/entertainment/2020/06/30/what-its-like-to-be-half-black-half-thai-morris-ks-story/

Lan, Shanshan. (2017). *Mapping the New African Diaspora in China. Race and the Cultural Politics of Belonging*. London: Routledge Press.

Lochery, Emma. (2012). 'Rendering Difference Visible: The Kenyan State and Its Somali Citizens,' *African Affairs*, 111 (44), pp. 615–39. doi: 10.1093/afraf/ads059

Malonde, Zamandulo. (2019). '"Druglocks" Mule Opens up About Trafficking and Drug Problems,' *Sowetan Live*, 6 August. Available at: https://www.sowetanlive .co.za/news/south-africa/2019-08-06-druglocks-mule-opens-up-about -trafficking-and-drug-problems/

Mangieri, Tina. (2007). *Refashioning South-South Spaces: Cloth, Clothing and Kenyan Cultures of Economies* (Doctoral dissertation). Chapel Hill: University of North Carolina.

Mathews, Gordon, Lin, Linessa Dan, & Yang, Yang. (2017). *The World in Guangzhou: Africans and Other Foreigners in South China's Global Marketplace*. Chicago: University of Chicago Press.

Mazrui, Ali. (2009). 'Preface: Comparative Africanity: Blood, Soil and Ancestry,' in Adibe, Jideofor (ed), *Who is an African? Identity, Citizenship and the Making of an Africa-Nation*, pp. 115–17. London: Adonis & Abbey.

Morris, James & Nguyen, Son. (2021). 'Nigerian and His Wife Led Romance Scam Gang that Generated ฿200 Million in 50 Accounts Since 2020,' *The Examiner .com*, 26 May. Available at: https://www.thaiexaminer.com/thai-news-foreigners /2021/05/26/nigerian-and-wife-in-200-million-baht-scam-gang/

Nyabvudzi, Tatenda & Chinyamurindi, Willie T. (2019). 'The Career Development Processes of Women Refugees in South Africa: An Exploratory Study,' *SA Journal of Industrial Psychology*, 45 (1), pp. 1–11.

Phaholtap, Hathairat. (2018). '"We Need to Survive," Syrians Escape Unending to Bangkok,' *Khaosod English*, 10 May. Available at: https://www.khaosodenglish .com/featured/2018/05/10/we-needed-to-survive-syrians-escape-war-unending -to-bangkok/

Spradley, James P. (1979). *The Ethnographic Interview*. Belmont: Cengage Learning.

Stebbins, Robert A. (2001). *Exploratory Research in Social Sciences*. Thousand Oaks: Sage Publications.

Sutthavong, Ariane. (2015). '24 Syrian Refugees Released on Bail,' *Bangkok Post*, 9 September. Available at: https://www.bangkokpost.com/thailand/general /685568/24-syrian-refugees-released-on-bail

Thaitrakulpanich, Asaree. (2020). 'Straight Outta Bangkok: What It's Like to be a Nigerian Rapper in Thailand,' *Khaosod English*, 8 July. Available at: https:// www.khaosodenglish.com/life/arts/2020/07/08/straight-outta-bangkok-what-its -like-to-be-a-nigerian-rapper-in-thailand/

Yalaz, Everen & Zapata-Barrero, Ricard. (2018). 'Mapping the Qualitative Migration Research in Europe: An Exploratory Analysis,' in Zapata-Borrero, Ricard & Yalaz, Everen (eds), *Qualitative Research in European Migration Studies*, pp. 9–33. Cham: Springer Press.

# 2 Africans in Thailand

## Mobility, race, and integration

*Elżbieta M. Goździak*

There are certain topics in migration studies that permeate not just scholarly discourses, but also policy debates and conversations among ordinary members of the host society. Immigrant integration is one such theme. Defined as the process of economic mobility and social inclusion, immigrant integration touches upon the policies, institutions, and mechanisms that promote development and growth within society. Successful integration builds communities that are economically stronger and more socially and culturally inclusive.

Immigrant integration is by no means an easy process. The immigrant experience has always been characterized by the tension between integration into the host society and preservation of ethnic identity and cultural heritage. Some migration scholars argue that the modern phenomena of multiculturalism and transnationalism diminish incentives for immigrants to participate in their new communities. Other scholars call for a reconceptualization of 'immigrant integration' (e.g., Crul 2016; Dahinden 2016; Korteweg 2017) or write against integration (Rytter 2019). Many policymakers claim that multiculturalism is ineffective precisely because it does not facilitate integration. Some even question whether very mobile individuals want to integrate. For immigrants, integration is also an issue of rights and obligations.

In order to contextualize the empirical research presented in this volume, I will focus on the issues of mobility and race as they pertain to the integration and belonging of Africans in Thailand. The concept of belonging is slowly replacing or being equated with integration. Belonging might also be understood in terms of balancing dual national attachments, which reveals the dynamic of identity processes and shows the similarities between integration and transnationalism (Erdal & Oeppen 2013).

Immigrant integration is widely debated in both scholarly and policy circles, but mostly in relation to migration movements from the Global South to Europe and North America (Freier & Holloway 2019). Even

DOI: 10.4324/9781003286554-2

though recent estimates suggest that a significant portion of international migration occurs in the southern hemisphere (Abel & Sander 2014), the topic of immigrant integration within South–South migration is rarely discussed.

Writing about South–South migration in West Africa, Jason Gagnoni and David Khoudour-Castérasi (2012) posit that the standard models of integration used in the North – assimilation and multiculturalism – are not necessarily applicable, because many migrants do not stay long enough to adopt local customs. On the other hand, they also argue that linguistic, cultural, and ethnic diversity tends to be higher in West Africa; therefore, basing immigrant integration on the multicultural premise may have little impact. They suggest that integration policies in the South should focus on the protection of migrant rights, while also fighting discrimination and fostering the incorporation of immigrants into society.

I would argue that Africans who work and live in Thailand are not mere sojourners. While they might want to remain mobile in order to conduct their trade, they also desire to expand their businesses and settle in Thailand. They certainly want to be integrated, not assimilated, both into the Thai economy and society. Protection of their rights is of great importance to them as well.

## Mobile foreigners, circular migrants, or immigrants?

Who are the Africans living in Thailand? The Thai Census Bureau classifies them as expatriates: persons living outside their country of origin or individuals living in a foreign country. This term corresponds with words of similar meaning, such as 'migrant' (a person who moves from one place to another in order to find work or better living conditions) or 'immigrant' (a person who comes to live permanently in a foreign country).

Some scholars portray Africans living and working in Thailand as classic circular migrants and argue that Africans practice circular migration to cope with immigration restrictions in Thailand. Furthermore, they argue that this translocal mobility reflects the fact that few Africans intend to settle permanently in Thailand. Supang Chantavanich posits that Africans' patterns of circular migration are similar to the migration of new Chinese investors and small traders coming to Thailand. The only difference is the scale of the migration. The new Chinese migrants known in Chinese language as *xin yi min* travel to Thailand as tourists and remain in the country for the duration of the tourist visa (90 days) to conduct small scale business. Much of their activity is aimed at serving Chinese tourists who visit Thailand annually in large numbers. In 2019, approximately 12 million Chinese tourists visited Thailand (Chantavanich 2021).

Most of the African entrepreneurs interviewed in the course of this research used to come to Thailand on 90-day tourist visas and travel to neighboring Laos or Cambodia to renew their visas often several times before they would return to Africa. However, changes in visa regulations that stipulated Africans renew visas in their home countries greatly affected their ability to use tourist visas to remain in the region and continue to do business in Thailand. Moreover, as our empirical data suggests, the process of renewing visas was a coping strategy resulting from a lack of other immigration provisions. It was not a part of planned circular migration. I argue that this strategy sets them apart from Chinese circular migrants.

Some Africans have remained in Thailand without proper documentation, but the vast majority of our interviewees hold business visas that allow them to lawfully work and live in Thailand (Unor & Thabchumpon, this volume). In some instances, business visas were acquired through marriage with a Thai citizen or partnership with a local Thai entrepreneur. Several of the interviewed Africans have lived in Thailand from anywhere between five and 17 years. Would the length of time spent in Thailand determine whether we call them circular migrants or immigrants?

I think a more productive strategy to theorize the journeys of Africans to Thailand is to look at the concepts used to debate cross-border movements. Currently, two-thirds of all international migrants originate in the Global South. For the majority of these migrants, a country in the Global South is also their destination. And yet, South–South migration is hardly ever theorized (Carling & Østbø Haugen 2020).

Most contemporary migration theories are based on immigration of Europeans to North America at the end of the 19th and the beginning of the 20th centuries. These theories regarded international migration as a unidirectional movement from country of origin to destination country that ended with settlement, usually permanent or at the very least long-term, or a permanent return home. When migrants returned home, the return was often considered to be a result of a 'failed migration project.' These theories no longer fit the mobile world we live in. They do not adequately conceptualize South–South movements, but they are also not effective in analyzing mobility within other continents.

Intra-European migration of Polish people is a perfect example to illustrate the inadequacies of the rather static migration theories of yesteryear. Contemporary trajectories of Polish migration became much more differentiated after the European Union enlargement and led to more diverse and floating populations. To paraphrase Bauman's work (2000, 2005) on 'liquid modernity,' Polish international migration has become 'liquid.' The concept of 'liquid migration' corresponds well with John Urry's work on mobilities (2007). Interestingly, Urry (2010) refers to another of Bauman's metaphors on 'gardening' (concerned with patterns, regularity, and ordering) versus 'gamekeeping' (regulating mobilities). He intimates that in the past, Eastern European societies used to be 'gardening' societies, but are now returning to the 'gamekeeper' phase with its fluid and complex networks and scapes.

Poles use their spatial mobility to adapt to the new context of post-communist space and EU enlargement. Rather than relying on transnational networking for improving their condition in the country of their settlement, many Poles tend to settle within mobility, staying mobile as long as they can in order to improve or maintain a particular quality of life, enhance their professional qualifications, and pursue educational goals. Their experience of migration becomes their lifestyle, their leaving home and going away, paradoxically, a strategy of staying at home, and, thus, an alternative to what international migration used to be considered: emigration or immigration.

For some Africans in Thailand, the 'settling into motion' trajectory is already a reality. African footballers who come to Thailand often envision their careers as very mobile since football is a global sport par excellence. Many footballers traverse continents and cross international borders in order to advance in their field and secure the best financial deal (Romero & Thammasaengadipha, this volume). For other migrants, the need to remain mobile is not always desirable. Many of the small traders in our studies found the need to go back to their home country to renew visas expensive and inconvenient. Their businesses and their lives are in Thailand. Still for others, 'settling into motion' was aspirational; they longed for visa provisions that would allow them to move between Thailand and their home country freely and without a need for constant visa renewals. A few of the protagonists presented in this volume also aspired to be able to travel to Kenya, where members of their extended families lived and participated in the clothes trading business. Gems traders, the majority of whom had business visas, have achieved the ability to travel in and out of Thailand, including selling gemstones in China. The business visas also allowed them to bring family members to Thailand (Vungsiriphisal, this volume).

Migration trajectories of the protagonists of our research very much depend on their individual circumstances and intersect with the political and/or economic situation in countries of origin, gender, age, and available resources. The interviewed migrants responded differently to push and pull factors. Khadija, Farooq, and Abdi fled Beledweyne in south-central Somalia, because they feared persecution by Al-Shabaab, a jihadist fundamentalist group, which attacks and terrorizes local populations. However, they chose different paths by which to come to Thailand: Khadija was smuggled, Farooq came as a student, and Abdi entered the country on a Kenyan passport (Kiarie, this volume). Are they circumstantial migrants?

Jørgen Carling and Heidi Østbø Haugen use the concept of circumstantial migration 'to describe migration trajectories and experiences that unfold in unpredictable ways under the influences of coincidence and micro-level context' (Carling & Østbø Haugen 2020: 2). Serendipity or coincidence did not play much of a role in the forced migration of Khadija, Farooq, and Abdi. There were elements of coincidence in the migration of some of the footballers, especially those who were not directly recruited from abroad, but rather relied on serendipitous meetings with coaches and other players. However, in all instances, the African migrants displayed a great deal of agency in planning their migration journey and adapting to local circumstances upon arrival in Thailand.

The types of mobility our protagonists pursued certainly diverged from the conventional teleological sequence of departure, arrival, settlement, and integration. A lot more research is needed to understand the complexity of migration from Africa to Thailand and to identify mobility patterns of Africans aspiring for better livelihoods in Thailand or seeking safe haven from persecution. I am not suggesting such research should result in an all-explaining, universal theory, but rather a multilayered taxonomy showing both the complexity of African migration to Thailand and the emerging regularities and patterns (de Haas 2021).

Let's now look briefly at the nexus of mobility and integration and consider the role mobility plays in integration and how it affects belonging.

## Integration and mobility

While some scholars argue that mobility and resulting trans- or even multilocality hinder integration processes (Chantavanich 2021), others contradict this assertion and emphasize the ways mobile people are grounded in multiple places (Smith 2001; Sinatti 2009) and identify with various places. Arjun Appadurai's construction of translocality rests on the assumption that the power of nation-states to command loyalty and identity is declining in a world of highly mobile subject formation (Appadurai 1995, 1996).

Many migrants talk about the fact that mobility is a significant part of their lives. The footballers and the gems traders discussed in this volume, in particular, stressed the importance of mobility and the significance of different places around the world to their careers. Arnoldo, originally from Angola, is also a naturalized citizen of Portugal, but has played football in several countries on different continents, including in Thailand. As a football player, he feels loyalty and attachment to the team with which he plays at any given time. He does not think that mobility narrows his integration and sense of belonging.

Indeed, mobility often extends the understanding of belonging and introduces multiple social, temporal, and spatial contexts of identification. According to Nira Yuval-Davies (2016), belonging becomes a multilayered and multiscalar process, which involves intersections of various social, cultural, economic, and political categories.

Currently, translocality is seen as a form of 'grounded transnationalism.' Furthermore, translocality highlights the extent to which the identity of a single place may be contested and in relying on dynamic connections to other places, never be completely bounded or territorialized (Mohan & Hughes 2020).

In summary, mobility can be empowering and can result in 'success.' It can become a tool for social innovation and agency as well as an important dimension of social capital provided that migrants retain control over their migration projects. In other words, it can result in successful integration and facilitate belonging in multiple places. Mobility, however, may also reflect increased dependencies, proliferation of precarious jobs, and labor exploitation that end in 'failure.' Whether it is a success or a failure depends as much on the economic background, educational, and social capital of the migrants as on the migration policies of the host country, including policies facilitating integration.

Thailand sorely lacks such policies not only for African migrants but also for migrant workers living and working in Thailand at the invitation of the Thai government. In a report based on the ILO/Japan Project on Managing Cross-border Movement of Labor in Southeast Asia, Pracha Vasuprasat (2010) suggests that Thailand should place immigration and labor migration policies high on its national agenda and promote social integration in Thailand. The author enumerates a range of barriers to cultural and social integration in Thai society and into the world of work that migrants experience. Unlike countries with well-planned immigration management, Thailand does not have any programs facilitating integration of migrant workers into its social, cultural, and working environments.

## Race and racism

Successful integration requires that immigrants have equal rights and necessary protections. Integration also necessitates immigrants are shown respect and are not discriminated against.

The 2007 Constitution of the Kingdom of Thailand guarantees equality of all persons and the prohibition of discrimination on the grounds of place of birth, race, language, gender, age, physical or health conditions, economic and social standing, religious belief, education, and political views (see Sections 4, 5, and 30 of the Thai Constitution). While the Constitution proclaims equality of all people, Thailand does not have any specific legislation on racial discrimination or hate speech (Permanent Mission of Thailand to the UN 2012).

Thailand ratified the *International Convention on the Elimination of All Forms of Racial Discrimination* in 2003, but it made an interpretative declaration that the country does not recognize 'any obligation beyond the confines of its constitution and law.' Additionally, Thailand did not accept Article 4 of the Convention, which stipulates the obligation to enact laws prohibiting the dissemination of all ideas based on racial superiority and hatred (hate speech), and Article 22, which confers on the International Court of Justice jurisdiction to deal with disputes concerning racial discrimination (Muntarbhorn 2012).

Given this state of affairs, the Convention's Committee on the Elimination of Racial Discrimination (CERD) called for legislation and procedures to protect refugees and asylum seekers in line with international human rights standards and more protection for migrant workers and advocated accession to the various treaties on refugees and reduction of statelessness (Muntarbhorn 2012).

These recommendations were made because racism and xenophobia are very visible in Thailand. Black people frequently face discrimination in the workplace and scrutiny from the police (Purnell 2013). Virtually every African migrant in our studies experienced discrimination (Unor & Thabchumpon, this volume; Issa, this volume). In the World Values Survey (2021), which measures attitudes on a variety of issues, 32.1 percent of Thai respondents said in 2018 that they would not like to have neighbors of a different race. Racist advertisements are also common place.

However, in the largely ethnically homogenous Thailand, many see racism as a Western issue, something that should be debated in multicultural societies like those in the United States or the United Kingdom. Thais argue that preference for light skin is a cosmetic issue that springs from a desire to look fashionable and wealthy and is not connected to a legacy of slavery, disenfranchisement, and marginalization. A distaste for black skin seems harmless to many Thais. This is, of course, deeply offensive to Black immigrants as well as to darker-complected Thais (Purnell 2013).

Some people excuse discriminatory attitudes towards African migrants emphasizing Thais' lack of familiarity with Black people. The first Black people the Thai society encountered were not Africans from the African continent, but African Americans, mainly airmen, stationed in Thailand beginning in April 1961 when an advance party of the US Air Force 6010th Tactical (TAC) Group arrived at Don Muang at the request of the Thai government to establish an aircraft warning system. The US Air Force presence grew rapidly with the expansion of the Laotian Civil War and the Vietnam War. At the height of the Vietnam War, some 50,000 American military personnel were stationed in Thailand; 10.6 percent were African Americans (Ruth 2017). Thais who remember those times speak of positive attitudes towards Black American soldiers. Unfortunately, the positive attitudes deteriorated as some of the American GIs engaged in drug abuse and prostitution.

Many of our interlocutors as well as the African researchers on our team thought that lack of familiarity with Black people is merely an excuse for Thais not to engage with the issue of racial discrimination. Our interlocutors' opinions correspond with postcolonial interventions which have shown that racism can no longer be taken as the attitude of uneducated or uninformed people and treated as a marginal and contingent phenomenon in the global system. Unfortunately, issues of race as well as gender and the colonial encounter which are at the center of debates in postcolonial studies elsewhere are routinely ignored by most Thai commentators (Persaud 2005).

Research on race and racism in Thailand has been conducted mainly by non-Thai scholars (e.g., Derks 2013; Draper et al. 2019; Jones 2016; Persaud 2005; Rackett 2019; Renard 2006; Weisman 2000; Zhuang 2014). Jan Weisman's anthropological investigations remain the principal, qualitative study of contemporary Thai racial discourse (2000). Peter Vandergeest (2003) investigated racialized spatial categories in regard to mountain peoples. Henry Delcore (2007) has similarly studied the racialization of Tai Lue and Lua relations in a northern Thai national park. There is also a fairly devastating first-person account of racial prejudices against a Black (Ethiopian) anthropologist working within the UN system in Thailand in the 1980s (Tegbaru 2020). According to John Draper and colleagues (2019), direct research into racial prejudice or discrimination in Thailand has recently been problematic, leading to personal harassment and threats to terminate research.

Thai racism operates at the nexus of several factors, including Thai Buddhist culture and worldview, and the concept of othering non-Thai people. In Thai Buddhist culture and worldview, the idea of fair skin is linked to modernity and its racial connotations are taken as being akin to Westernness, as Jan Weisman (1997: 59) writes:

> Modernization, Westernization, and internationalization are thus seen by Thais as processes in which one strives towards goals that are invariably represented by images of White people. At the same time, images of Blacks are taken to represent the denigrated conditions away from which Thai development should move.

In Thai Buddhist worldview, physical characteristics have traditionally been considered key signifiers of one's accumulated merit: 'Clarity of complexion, grace, and serenity were reflections of moral goodness … Ugliness, unfortunately, conveyed the opposite' (Van Esterik 1999: 12). The idea that black is ugly and white is beautiful seems to stem from the notion that darker skin represents a life of manual labor in the sun and therefore a lower social class with a lack of money and education and that light skin is a sign of privilege (Persaud 2005).

In Thailand, treatment of darker-complected individuals, including African migrants, is clearly based on exclusionary principles of race. As Tim Racket (2019) reminds us, Thais identify Malay Muslims as *khaek*, a category that subsumes multiple ethnicities (South Asians, Malays, Arabs) aggregated together by the shared attribute of having dark skin. Thais use skin color as a means for inclusion or exclusion. A dark complexion can be read by Buddhists as a sign of impurity and inner badness (Jerryson 2011). Thus, it is not ethnicity that is a root cause of racism, exclusion, and inequality in Thai society but, rather, how race and religion are combined in identity formation.

Creating the Other requires defining Thainess against which the Other can exist (Renard 2006). What constitutes Thainess? Thai anthropologist Pinkaew Laungaramsri (2003: 157) asserts that Thainess is a 'collective identity [...] constituted by shared commonality of language, religion and monarchy' as shaped by the need 'to be loyal to [those] three principles/pillars.' All the country's diverse peoples are expected to practice cultural traits that the state has identified as 'Thai.' Thai citizenship is also defined as being 'Thai.' Although the Thai Constitution allows for choice of religion, many people in Thailand believe strongly that Thais must be Buddhist. In fact, only the King has to be Buddhist.

The national language promoted by the government is the Thai spoken by the upper classes of central Thailand. As a result, many hill people of Thailand have been institutionally excluded from membership in the nation-state. Many hill people born in the country as well as those who migrated to Thailand do not have Thai citizenship. Among the six Greater Mekong Region countries, Thailand alone has no clear policy defining minority groups as citizens (Renard 2006). Things are changing albeit slowly. Citizenship was granted to some hill tribe people in order to eradicate opium growing (Anderson 2017).

I could go on and provide many more examples of othering minorities and migrants in Thailand. All of our African interlocutors talked about being othered by landlords, employers, neighbors, and even customers (see Unor & Thabchumpon; Issa, this volume). We have heard testimonies that African children in Thai schools are called names and are not easily accepted by both classmates and teachers (Vungsiripaisal, this volume). Attitudes towards the racialized Other affect the ability of migrants to integrate into Thai society and feel that they belong. As Fatma Issa (this volume) documented, many Somali asylum seekers try to become invisible to avoid discrimination and xenophobia.

## Integration and belonging at the intersection of racial othering

Given the level of racial discrimination, xenophobia, and othering, it is difficult to be optimistic about the prospects for migrant integration, especially Black migrants. The position of the Thai government also does not bode well for African migrants.

In 2009, speaking at the launch of the United Nations Development Program (UNDP) report on migration, former Prime Minister Abhisit Vejjajiva noted that:

> Migration … is an expression of the freedom and desire of each individual to seek better opportunities in life, mostly through the exercise of basic human rights, the pursuit of peace, education and employment. As 'Thailand' means 'the land of the free,' it is our government's policy to ensure that migrants can enjoy *their* freedom and social welfare in Thailand while *their* human rights are duly respected.
>
> (Vejjajiva 2009; emphasis added by Dreks 2013)

Analyzing his speech, Annushka Derks (2013) concluded that by virtue of not being 'Thai,' migrants are excluded from privileges commonly associated with being 'Thai.' They simply do not have the right to have rights.

This attitude corresponds with the primordial understanding of belonging based on notions of shared culture and ascribed identity (Hartnell 2006). This understanding is often (Bellamy 2004), although not necessarily (Franck 1996), synonymous with nationalism. The primordial view is associated with legal norms against dual nationality although in reality, dual or even multiple citizenship has become a widespread phenomenon in many parts of the world (Blatter 2011).

Belonging can also be understood in terms of balancing between dual national attachments, which reveals the dynamic of identity processes and shows the similarities between integration and transnationalism (Erdal & Oeppen 2013). I would also argue that belonging is not singular, but rather plural (Pawlak & Goździak 2019). It includes meaningful relations with different social, cultural, and material surroundings. Since migration often includes changes and transformations in migrants' lives, belonging cannot be understood as fixed. Belonging is constantly re-negotiated by migrants and depends on local circumstances as well as spatial and temporal aspects of migration strategies (see Bradatan et al. 2010; Saar 2018). This is especially true about very mobile migrants.

I think the Thai government and Thai society need to realize this complexity and conditionality of migrants' attachment to different places. Migration scholars, especially those based in Thailand, should study experiential, practical, and affective aspects of belonging (and unbelonging), which intersect with mobility, social class, and gender of African migrants.

## Conclusions

Although South–South migration is on the rise, migration policy in the Global South is remarkably underdeveloped (Bakewell et al. 2009). In the North, policy-makers and scholars are concerned about migration management, i.e., the control of entry and issues of settlement, including social, economic, political, and cultural integration, multiculturalism, racism, community cohesion, and xenophobia. In contrast, the debates in the South are more concerned with issues of emigration, 'brain drain,' impact of migration on development, remittances, and the role of migrants and their descendants in the development of the country of origin.

Thai (and other Asian) policy-makers continue to focus on temporary migrant workers who are not expected to settle in Thailand. Employers want low-skilled and low-paid workers to meet immediate labor needs and pay no attention to integration issues. They and the general public do not think migrants belong in Thai society. The prevailing sentiment among policy-makers in Thailand (and elsewhere in Asia) is that immigration is not good for the nation-state and should only be a temporary expedient; migration policies should be concerned mainly with restrictions; immigrants should not be allowed to settle; foreign residents should not normally be offered citizenship; national culture and identity should not be modified in response to external influences (Castles 2004; Skeldon 2006). Ideas from Europe, North America, or Oceania on the benefits of multiculturalism are unpopular in Thailand and most Asian countries, and turning immigrants into citizens is unthinkable.

However, a key question for the future is whether this exclusionary model, based on race, can be sustained in the face of demographic and economic trends which encourage more labor migration, longer stay, and family reunion.

Whether Africans (or other migrants) settle in Thailand permanently or remain mobile and traverse between Africa and Asia, it seems important to develop integration policies and programs to ensure their protection, accord them appropriate rights (and obligations), and facilitate their integration into the economic and social sphere. In the globalized world, we all need to belong.

# References

Abel, Gut J. & Nikola Sander. (2014). 'Quantifying global international migration flows,' *Science*, 343 (6178), pp. 1520–1522.

Anderson, Bobby. (2017). 'People, Land and Poppy: The Political Ecology of Opium and the Historical Impact of Alternative Development in Northwest Thailand,' *Forest and Society*, 1 (1), pp. 48–59.

Appadurai, Arjun. (1995). 'The Production of Locality,' in Fardon, R (ed), *Counterworks: Managing the Diversity of Knowledge*, pp. 208–209. London: Routledge.

Appadurai, Arjun. (1996). *Modernity at Large: Cultural Dimensions of Globalization*. Minneapolis: University of Minnesota Press.

Bauman, Zygmunt. (2000). *Liquid Modernity*. Cambridge: Polity.

Bauman, Zygmunt. (2005). *Liquid Life*. Cambridge: Polity.

Bakewell, Oliver, de Haas, Hein, Castles, Stephen, Vezzoli, Simona, & Jónsson, Gunvor. (2009). 'South-South Migration and Human Development: Reflections on African Experiences,' *Human Development Research Paper 2009/07*. https://www.migrationinstitute.org/publications/wp-15-09

Bellamy, Richard. (2004). 'Introduction: The Making of Modern Citizenship,' in Bellamy, R., Castiglione, D., & Santoro, E. (eds), *Lineages of European Citizenship: Rights, Belonging and Participation in Eleven Nation States*, pp. 1–21. New York: Palgrave Macmillan.

Blatter, Joachim. (2011). 'Dual Citizenship and Theories of Democracy,' *Citizenship Studies*, 15 (6–7), pp. 769–98.

Bradatan, Cristina, Popan, Adrian, & Melton, Rachel. (2010). 'Transnationality as a fluid social identity,' *Social Identities*, 16 (2), pp. 169–78.

Carling, Jørgen & Heidi Østbø Haugen. (2020). 'Circumstantial Migration: How Gambian Journeys to China Enrich Migration Theory,' *Journal of Ethnic and Migration Studies*, 47 (12), pp. 2778–95. doi: 10.1080/1369183X.2020.1739385

Castes, Stephen. (2004). 'The Myth of the Controllability of Difference: Labor Migration, Transnational Communities and State Strategies in the Asia-Pacific Region,' in Yeoh, B. S. A. & Willis, K. (eds), *State/Nation/Transnation: Perspectives on Transnationalism in the Asia-Pacific*. London: Routledge.

Chantavanich, Supang. (2021). 'China's Rising Influence in Thailand: Translocal Human Mobility and its Impact,' in Chirathiwat, Suthiphand, Rutchatorn, Buddhagarn, & Nakawiroj, Wasutadorn (eds), *China's Rise in Mainland ASEAN: Regional Evidence and Local Responses*, pp. 133–54. Bangkok: World Scientific.

Crul, Maurice. (2016). 'Super-diversity vs. Assimilation: How Complex Diversity in Majority–Minority Cities Challenges the Assumptions of Assimilation,' *Journal of Ethnic and Migration Studies*, 42 (1), pp. 54–68.

Dahinden, J. (2016). 'A Plea for the 'De-migranticization' of Research on Migration and Integration,' *Ethnic and Racial Studies*, 39 (13), pp. 2207–25.

de Haas, Hans. (2021). 'A Theory of Migration: The Aspirations-capabilities Framework,' *Comparative Migration Studies*, 9 (8). doi: 10.1186/s40878-020-00210-4

Delcore, Henry H. (2007). 'The Racial Distribution of Privilege in a Thai National Park,' *Journal of Southeast Asian Studies*, 38 (1), pp. 83–105.

Derks, Annuska. (2013). 'Human Rights and (Im)mobility: Migrants in the State of Thailand,' *Sojourn*, 28 (2), pp. 216–40.

Draper, John, Sobieszczyk, Teresa, Crumpton, Charles David, Lefferts, H. L. & Chachavalpongpun, Pavin. (2019). 'Racial "Othering" in Thailand: Quantitative Evidence, Causes, and Consequences,' *Nationalism and Ethnic Politics*, 25 (3), pp. 251–72.

Erdal, Marta Bivand & Oeppen, Ceri. (2013). 'Migrant Balancing Acts: Understanding the Interactions Between Integration and Transnationalism,' *Journal of Ethnic and Migration Studies*, 39 (6), pp. 867–84.

Franck, Thomas M. (1996). 'Clan and Superclan: Loyalty, Identity and Community in Law and Practice.' *The American Journal of International Law*, 90 (3), pp. 359–383. https://doi.org/10.2307/2204063.

Freier, Louisa F. & Holloway, Kyle. (2019). 'The Impact of Tourist Visas on Intercontinental South–South Migration: Ecuador's Policy of 'Open Doors' as a Quasi-Experiment,' *International Migration Review*, 53 (4), pp. 1171–1208.

Gagnon, Jason & Khoudour-Castéras, David. (2012). 'South-South Migration in West Africa: Addressing the Challenge of Immigrant Integration,' *OECD Development Centre Working Papers* (312). Paris: OECD Publishing. doi: 10.1787/5k98p4wcgjmx-en

Hartnell, Helen E. (2006). 'Belonging: Citizenship and Migration in the European Union and in Germany,' *Berkeley Journal of International Law*, 330, pp. 330–400.

Jerryson, Michael K. (2011). *Buddhist Fury: Religion and Violence in Southern Thailand*. New York: Oxford University Press.

Jones, Kristina. (2016). 'An Insight into Thailand's Construction of the Thai Race, Identity and Consequent Thainess,' *CERS Working Paper*.

Korteweg, Anna C. (2017). 'The Failures of "Immigrant Integration": The Gendered Racialized Production of Non-belonging,' *Migration Studies*, 5 (3), pp. 428–44.

Laungaramsri, Pinkaew. (2003). 'Ethnicity and the Politics of Ethnic Classification in Thailand,' In *Ethnicity in Asia*, edited by Mackerras, Colin. London: Routledge Curzon.

Mohan, Urmila & Hughes, Jessica. (2020). '2020 Special Issue: Translocality and Connections that Disrupt,' *The Jugaad Project*, 14 July. Available at: https://www.thejugaadproject.pub/home/translocality-as-connections

Muntarbhorn, Vitit. (2012). 'Thailand's Race Laws Face Scrutiny,' *Bangkok Post*, 5 September. Available at: https://www.bangkokpost.com/opinion/opinion/310876/thailand-race-laws-face-scrutiny

Pawlak, Marek & Goździak, Elżbieta M. (2019). 'Multiple Belongings: Transnational Mobility, Social Class, and Gendered Identities among Polish Migrants in Norway,' *Social Identities*, 26 (1), pp. 77–91. doi: 10.1080/13504630.2019.1677458

Permanent Mission of Thailand to the UN. (2012). *Questionnaire Pursuant to Human Rights Council (HRC) Resolution A/HRC/21/30*. Available at: https://www.ohchr.org/Documents/Issues/Racism/AdHoc/5thsession/Thailand.pdf

Persaud, Walter. (2005). 'Gender, Race and Global Modernity: A Perspective from Thailand,' *Globalizations*, 2 (2), pp. 210–27.

Purnell, Newley. (2013). 'Images Spark Racism Debate in Thailand,' *The New Yorker*, 31 October. Available at: https://www.newyorker.com/business/currency/images-spark-racism-debate-in-thailand

Rackett, Tim. (2019). 'Who Do They Think You Are? Imagined Ethnic and Religious Identities, Thai Racism and Violence in Southern Thailand,' *Human Rights and*

*Peace in Southeast Asia Series*, 4, pp. 93–109. Available at: https://shapesea.com/publication/human-rights-in-southeast-asia-series-four-challenging-the-norms/

Renard, Ronald D. (2006). 'Creating the Other Requires defining Thainess Against Which the Other Can Exist: Early-Twentieth Century Definitions,' *Southeast Asian Studies*, 44 (3), pp. 295–320.

Ruth, Richard A. (7 November 2017). "Why Thailand Takes Pride in the Vietnam War" (Editorial). *New York Times*.

Rytter, Mikkel. (2019). 'Writing Against Integration: Danish Imaginaries of Culture, Race and Belonging,' *Ethnos*, 84 (4), pp. 678–97. doi: 10.1080/00141844.2018.1458745

Saar, Maarja. (2018). 'To Return or Not to Return? The Importance of Identity Negotiations for Return Migration,' *Social Identities*, 24 (1), pp. 20–133. doi: 10.1080/13504630.2017.1310038

Sinatti, Giulia. (2009). Home Is Where the Heart Abides. Migration, Return and Housing in Dakar, Senegal. *Open House International*, 34, pp. 49–56. 10.1108/OHI-03-2009-B0006.

Skeldon, Ronald. (2006). 'Interlinkages Between Internal and International Migration and Development in the Asian Region,' *Population, Space and Place*, 12 (1), pp. 15–30.

Tegbaru, Amare. (2020). 'The Racialization of Development Expertise and the Fluidity of Blackness: A Case from 1980s Thailand,' *Asian Anthropology*, 19 (3), pp. 195–212. doi: 10.1080/1683478X.2020.1713288

Urry, John. (2007). *Mobilities*. Cambridge: Polity Press.

Urry, John. (2010). 'Mobile World,' *British Journal of Sociology*, 61 (1) Supplement 1, pp. 347–66. doi: 10.1111/j.1468-4446.2009.01249.x

Van Esterik, Penny. (1999). 'Repositioning Gender, Sexuality, and Power in Thai Studies,' in Jackson, Peter A. & Cook, Nerida M. (eds), *Genders and Sexualities in Modern Thailand*, pp. 275–89. Chiang Mai: Silkworm Books

Vandergeest, Peter. (2003). 'Racialization and Citizenship in Thai Forest Politics,' *Society and Natural Resources*, 16 (1), pp. 19–37.

Vasuprasat, Pracha. (2010). 'Agenda for Labor Migration Policy in Thailand: Towards Long-term Competitiveness,' *ILO/Japan Project on Managing Cross-border Movement of Labor in Southeast Asia; ILO Regional Office for Asia and the Pacific*. Bangkok: ILO.

Weisman, Jan R. (1997). 'Rice Outside the Paddy: The Form and Function of Hybridity in a Thai Novel,' *Crossroads: An Interdisciplinary Journal of Southeast Asian Studies*, 11 (1), pp. 51–78.

Weisman, Jan R. (2000). *Tropes and Traces: Hybridity, Race, Sex, and Responses to Modernity in Thailand* (Doctoral dissertation). Washington: University of Washington.

World Values Survey. (2021). *Wave 7 (2017–2020) Thailand*. Available at: https://www.worldvaluessurvey.org/WVSDocumentationWV7.jsp

Yuval-Davies, Nira. (2016). 'Power, Intersectionality and the Politics of Belonging,' in Harcourt, W. (ed), *The Palgrave Handbook of Gender and Development*, pp. 367–81. Basingstoke: Palgrave Macmillan.

Zhuang, Kuansong. (2001). To race or not to race?–The (De)Racialization of the Thai in History. CERS Working Paper.

# 3 'Good guys in, bad guys out'

## Thailand's immigration policy and perceptions of African immigrants

*Supang Chantavanich and
Waranya Jitpong*

## Introduction

Writing about African migrants in Thailand is not an easy task given the limited statistical data and non-existing empirical research (Goździak, this volume). Africans constitute a small but growing percentage of migrants in the country. According to the Thai Immigration Office, a record number of Africans – 236,338 persons – arrived in Thailand in 2019. However, this number represents but six percent of all the foreign travelers – 40.37 million – who came to Thailand in 2019. The majority of foreign visitors to Thailand are tourists. In 2019, 39.8 million tourists visited Thailand, including 96,499 South Africans (Thailand Embassy in Pretoria Factsheet 2019). There are also foreign investors and business people who frequently visit the country.

This chapter provides a policy context against which migration, both forced and economic, from Africa to Thailand unfolds. We present and analyze immigration policies that facilitate or impede settlement of Africans in Thailand. A brief mapping of the different groups of Africans currently residing in Thailand follows. We end the chapter with policy recommendations aimed at immigration authorities and other branches of the Thai government responsible for foreigners residing in the country.

This chapter is informed by interviews with immigration authorities and narcotics suppression staff in the Bureau of the Royal Thai Police, a former Thai ambassador to South Africa, and the Thai embassy staff in Pretoria, as well as civil society organizations working with African asylum seekers and urban refugees in Thailand. All interviews were conducted in Thai. Interviews with immigration officials focused on the Immigration Act of 1979 and subsequent decrees. Some interviews were face-to-face and some were by phone. We have also reviewed unpublished statistical information the interviewees shared with us as well as published immigration orders.

DOI: 10.4324/9781003286554-3

We were particularly interested in the implementation of immigration policies vis-à-vis African migrants. This issue was of interest because many African migrants claim that they are being discriminated against by immigration officials and the police. There is evidence, reported in the media, that there were continuous raids and arrests of African migrants in Thailand especially between 2016 and 2018 (Mokkhasen 2016; Ngamkham 2017; Daily News 2017; Prachatai 2019; Saksornchai 2018).

We discuss the Thai Immigration Act of 1979, outline the different visa categories, discuss refugee and asylum policies, explain the 'good guys in, bad guys out' policy and its impact, and conclude with policy recommendations aimed at making the Thai immigration regime more coherent and responsive to both humanitarian emergencies and labor shortages.

## Thailand's migration policy

The Thai Immigration Act of 1927 controlled travel to/from Thailand during the absolute monarchy (Immigration Bureau 2020a). In the aftermath of World War II, crises and conflicts in neighboring countries caused Thai immigration policy to be more restrictive (OECD/ ILO 2017). In the 1950s and beyond, Thailand did not encourage immigration (Chantavanich 1999). The policy changed during the 1970–80s when the nation became both an emigration and immigration country and the new Immigration Act of 1979 was launched (Thailand Immigration Act 1979), requiring arrivals to have a valid passport and an appropriate visa.

## Thailand's visa regime

The Immigration Act of 1979 established four major types of visas: tourist, business, diplomatic, and non-immigrant visas. Tourists are allowed to visit the country for a period of 30 days with the possibility of extending their stay up to 90 days (Immigration Bureau 2020b). Those who apply for a business visa must adhere to the Investment Promotion Act of 1977 (amended 2001) of the Ministry of Commerce (Thailand Investment Promotion Act 1977). Currently, there are six different categories of visas for temporary stay: (1) Transit, (2) Tourist, (3) Non-immigrant, (4) Diplomatic, (5) Official, and (6) Courtesy. Non-immigrant visas include Business (B), Business Approved (B-A), Investment (IB), Teaching (B), and Long Stay (O-A) (Ministry of Foreign Affairs 2019a). Non-immigrant visas apply also to athletes, airline/port/station crew, students, media journalists, missionaries, scientists /researchers/trainers/teachers, and skilled artists. Visas for low-wage labor migrants from Cambodia, Laos, and Myanmar are not included in these categories.

Nationals of 64 countries, including South Africa and Mauritius, with bilateral reciprocal arrangements, are exempt from visa requirements. Consequently, many tourists from South Africa and Mauritius visit Thailand every year, but they are mainly non-Black citizens of those countries. Additionally, visitors from certain countries may apply for visa-on-arrival for short-term stays. Foreigners entering Thailand are not permitted to work without a work permit but may seek employment while in the country. Many African footballers studied by Romero and Thammasaengadipha (this volume) came to Thailand on tourist visas to seek employment.

There is nothing in the Thai immigration legislation akin to the US 'green card' or the Canadian 'landed immigrant' status that allows migrants to immigrate and settle permanently in Thailand. Foreigners who meet certain requirements can obtain a permanent residence status (Immigration Bureau 2020b), but that must be extended annually. Some non-immigrant visas can be extended annually.

## Thailand's labor migration policy

Since the 1990s, labor migrants have constituted the largest number of migrants in Thailand. According to a study conducted jointly by the Singapore Management University (SMU) and JP Morgan, Thailand has faced a shortage of qualified technical and vocational workers across all industries. These shortages are due to inability of tertiary education to keep pace with industry demands and a cultural bias towards a more academic education. The shortage of skilled workers is especially acute in the automotive, information and communications technology (ICT), and tourism sectors (The Nation 2016). Despite these shortages, there are no special immigrant or non-immigrant visas aimed at bringing in the needed labor force. Instead, there is a patchwork of *ad hoc* provisions for different types of migrant workers.

The government revised its former Alien Employment Act 1978 (Thailand Alien Employment Permit Act 1978) and issued a new decree in 2017 to handle both high-skill and low-skill migrant workers. This scheme requires more complex processes such as an Annual Income Tax Declaration Form for the previous year and an official letter that certifies registration of a person or enterprise as a legal entity. Additionally, a regulation requires foreigners visiting, living, or working in Thailand to report their place of residence every 90 days (Bruton 2019).

Thailand has signed Memoranda of Understanding (MOUs) with Laos, Cambodia, Myanmar, and Vietnam to import low-skill labor in the fishing, agriculture, construction, manufacturing, domestic work, and other service sectors (Grimwade & Neumann 2019). A study by the International

Labor Organization (ILO) and Organization for Economic Co-operation Development (OECD) indicated that migrants were responsible for 4.3 to 6.6 percent of Thailand's GDP in 2010, while representing only 4.7 percent of the employed population (OECD/ILO 2017). Africans and other Asians are not eligible for the employment schemes devised by the Thai government.

While privileging labor migrants from the sub-region, Thai immigration policy excludes migrants from low-income countries anywhere else in the world. Thai authorities often cite the three principles that guide their immigration policy, namely national security, protection of work opportunities for Thai citizens, and support of regional development (Hall 2011). Thailand's immigration provisions are not very different from immigration policies in other Association of Southeast Asian Nations (ASEAN) countries. As an exception, Singapore immigration policy favors high-skill migrant workers, techno-entrepreneurs, and investors, while excluding/marginalizing low-skill migrant workers (Yeoh 2006). Singapore is the only country in ASEAN that grants citizenship to foreigners, especially professionals who come to work locally (Sucharitkul 1990).

## Refugee policy, a delicate matter

The Thai government is not a signatory to the 1951 *UN Convention on Refugees* or the 1967 *Protocol Relating to the Status of Refugees*. Despite hosting more than a million refugees in the aftermath of the Vietnam War, the Thai government criticized the *Refugee Convention* and the *Protocol* for not requiring international cooperation or addressing the root causes of refugee displacement (Severson 2020). Additionally, Thailand has always feared that massive local settlement of refugees and migrants would pose a serious threat to the country's national security. The issue of refugees as a security threat has been contested (Goździak 2021; Kerwin 2016), but many governments still believe that refugees and immigrants are a threat to both national security and social cohesion of their countries (Goździak et al. 2020).

When Thailand hosted large numbers of Indochinese refugees fleeing the Vietnam War, the Thai government always reminded the international community that it might resort to forced repatriation if voluntary repatriation and/or third-country resettlement failed (Pongsapich & Chongwatana 1988). International civil society groups and media thought the decision not to ratify the Refugee Convention arbitrary, and the indefinite detention and *refoulement* of some asylum seekers, including Uyghurs from Xinjiang China, unjustified (Human Rights Watch 2017, Colbey 2018).

Not being a signatory of the Refugee Convention means that the Thai government has no legally binding obligations toward asylum seekers and refugees (Dewansyah & Handayani 2018). However, Thailand has used the available legal frameworks, such as the Immigration Act of 1979, to accommodate arriving refugees and asylum seekers (Panprom 2020). Under this law, asylum seekers in Thailand are technically 'illegal immigrants,' subject to arrest, detention, or deportation. However, under the same legislation, the Ministry of the Interior (MOI) with the approval of the Cabinet and the National Security Council may allow foreigners to stay temporarily in Thailand (Chantavanich & Reynolds 1988). In other words, refugee reception is considered at state discretion based on immigration laws and policies that show state sovereignty in security issues, rather than a human right-based approach (Dewansyah & Handayani 2018). In dealing with 'displaced persons' (an official term for refugees), the Thai government has adopted four solutions: encampment, responsibility sharing, resettlement, and repatriation (Chantavanich 2011). These *ad hoc* provisions have been used in the past and continue to be deployed now. After the fall of Saigon in 1975, Thailand received more than one million refugees from Cambodia, Laos, and Vietnam. Between 1975 and 1986, the Indochinese refugees remained in refugee camps at the border until appropriate durable solutions, particularly resettlement and repatriation, were achieved at a later date (Chantavanich 2011). By 1993, the Cambodian repatriation was completed (Lang 2001).

In recent decades, refugees fleeing armed conflict in Myanmar sought safe haven in Thailand. Using the same *ad hoc* provision, the government allowed asylum seekers from Myanmar to stay in border shelters and receive humanitarian support (Chantavanich 2011). Thai policy referred to these individuals as 'displaced persons fleeing fighting' (rather than 'refugees') and housed them in 'temporary shelters' (rather than 'refugee camps'). Their official immigration status remained 'illegal entrant' (Lang 2001). In the early 1990s, Thailand admitted another group of 'displaced persons from Myanmar,' i.e., Rohingya (Vungsiriphisal et al. 2014). The Rohingya included both refugees and victims of human trafficking as well as some economic migrants (Chantavanich 2020). The policy provides for 'temporary shelter' and a promise that Thailand will not deport asylum seekers until the conditions in their country of origin improve (Lang 2001).

Adam Severson (2020) aptly described Thai policies toward asylum seekers and refugees as anchored in vague 'humanitarian' principles and protean – by turn hospitable and hostile – guided by a mixture of humanitarian beneficence, securitization, political expedience, and qualified respect for international norms. Indeed, this mixture of positive and negative features characterized the Thai government's response to refugees ever since the arrival of large numbers of refugees from Vietnam, Laos, and Cambodia after the fall of Saigon.

## Changing landscape of asylum policy

Many scholars and refugee advocates agree that the Thai 1979 Immigration Act is inadequate to respond to asylum seekers' claims and protect human rights of the displaced (Jones 2015). Reliance on the Immigration Act has limited Thailand's ability to take responsibility for refugees and asylum seekers.

In the absence of a government mechanism, the United Nations High Commissioner for Refugees (UNHCR)-Bangkok has screened 'urban' asylum seekers using a process known as 'refugee status determination' (RSD). RSD has been costly and controversial, and UNHCR has long lobbied the Thai government for a permanent, government-administered process.

Between 2015 and 2017, Asylum Access Thailand (AAT), a legal aid organization in Bangkok, served more than 500 African asylum seekers, mainly from Somalia. In 2017 and 2018, AAT submitted 2,431 asylum applications, including 257 on behalf of African asylum seekers. Asylum seekers from Pakistan constituted half of all asylum seekers, while Somalis dominated asylum seekers from Africa. However, few were successful in obtaining refugee status (Issa, this volume).

UNHCR continues to screen urban refugees. Table 3.1 shows the number of urban refugees registered with UNHCR in 2017 and 2018. In 2019,

*Table 3.1* Number of African Urban Refugees in Thailand 2017–18

| 2017 | | 2018 | |
|---|---|---|---|
| Country of origin | Number of urban refugees | Country of origin | Number of urban refugees |
| Somalia | 223 | Somalia | 230 |
| Congo | 33 | Congo | 21 |
| Egypt | 16 | Egypt | 15 |
| Ivory Coast | 16 | Ivory Coast | 15 |
| Sudan | 14 | Ethiopia | 13 |
| Ethiopia | 13 | Sudan | 12 |
| Eritrea | 8 | Eritrea | 7 |
| Zimbabwe | 8 | Togo | 6 |
| Togo | 5 | | |
| Total African urban refugees | 336 | | 319 |
| Total urban refugees (all nationalities) | 3,962 | | 4,292 |
| Percent of African urban refugees | 8.48 | | 7.43 |

Source: Asylum Access Thailand.

Note: Countries with fewer than four refugees – Burundi, Cameroon, Gambia, Guinea, Liberia, Mali, Morocco, Niger, Senegal, Tanzania – are not included.

there were 5,070 urban refugees and asylum seekers from all nationalities in Thailand (UNHCR 2000).

During the 2016 *Summit on the Global Refugee Crisis* in New York, Thai Prime Minister Prayut Chan-o-cha pledged to end the detention of refugee children. He also promised that Thailand would develop guidelines to formally protect refugees in Thailand (Alastair 2018). A year later, in 2017, the Thai government formalized the screening procedure for asylum seekers. In 2019, the Immigration Bureau set up a new division to work collaboratively with UNHCR to screen asylum applications and issue refugee cards to eligible applicants (interview with Immigration Police October 7, 2019).

In 2019, three regulations were issued to clarify Thai asylum policy:

1) *Ministerial Regulation on the Screening of Aliens Entering Thailand who Cannot Return to Place of Origin (2019)*, Office of the Prime Minister;
2) Regulation on the Role and Responsibility of Divisions in the *Immigration Bureau* (National Police Office 2019);
3) *Note on Endorsement of the Immigration Police to Take Role and Responsibility in Screening Asylum Seekers According to the Ministerial Regulation on the Screening of Aliens Entering Thailand and Cannot Return to Place of Origin (2019)*, Office of the Prime Minister, endorsed by the Edict Office (Unpublished document, the Edict Office 2019).

The first document defined standard operating procedures (SOP) for asylum seeker screening and established a screening committee with the Head Commander of the Police Bureau as chair. A new division was established in the Immigration Bureau to handle the screening process in consultation with UNHCR and in accordance with the *nonrefoulement* principle. The note from the Edict Office legally endorses the role and responsibility of the Immigration Bureau to improve refugee protections (Park 2020).

The new refugee screening mechanism was scheduled to take effect by June 22, 2020. However, the deadline was missed, presumably because of COVID-19. At the time of this writing, the Thai government has not released a new timeline for the implementation of the screening mechanism.

## '*Good guys in, bad guys out*:' Perceptions and immigration regulations affecting Africans

'*Good guys in, bad guys out*' was the message from Pol. Lt. Gen. Nathathorn Prousoontorn, Immigration Bureau Commissioner, as immigration officials prepared to launch the Bureau's 2016 crackdown on visa overstayers (Hua Hin 2016). However, based on implementation of the policy, immigration police seemed to consider Africans, *de facto*, to be 'bad guys.' The African migrants interviewed by the contributors to this volume definitely felt discriminated against and targeted by the Thai authorities (Ukam Unor & Thabchumpon, this volume).

Although Thai immigration laws do not overtly discriminate against any particular group, we posit that the police often stereotype and target Black Africans (and dark-complected South Asians). There are several reasons Thailand does not welcome African migrants. First, African migrants are generally from low-income countries and are not the big investors that Thailand wants to attract, especially in the high-tech industries. The majority of foreign investors in Thailand are from Japan, the European Union, and the United States (Immigration Statistics 2020). Second, some Africans living in Thailand were involved in high-profile cases of drug trafficking and other criminal activities in the past (Chavalit 2016). Third, the rising numbers of asylum seekers from West African countries have unsettled the Thai authorities. While Thai immigration officials claim to treat asylum seekers and refugees registered with UNHCR no differently than others (Quinley 2019), African refugees seem to suffer more from racial profiling (Jones 2015; Son 2018).

## 'Good guys:' Investors, traders, athletes, and students

Thailand's efforts to break into African markets are in line with a series of re-engagements by countries of the Global South in Africa. China and India are leading the way, followed by South Korea, Indonesia, and Japan (Haugen Østbø 2018). Thailand opened a new diplomatic chapter focusing on Africa as part of the 'Look West Policy.' The Thai–Africa Initiative was launched in 2013, and by 2017, the Initiative was elevated to the Thai–Africa Partnership for Sustainable Development with the Thailand International Cooperation Agency (TICA) (Tarrosy 2018).

Among ASEAN countries, Thailand ranks number one for exporting automobile parts, rice, rubber tires, and canned/processed seafood to Africa. In return, Thailand imports aluminum, chemical products, gold, diamonds, platinum, paper pulp, and steel from Africa. In 2019, Thailand–Sub-Saharan Africa trade was valued at $2,727,961.38, including $5,146,423.16 in exports and $2,418,461.78 in imports (World Integrated Trade Solution 2019). However, the ease of Thai investment in Africa does not seem to be reciprocated.

African nations investing in Thailand include, principally, South Africa, Nigeria, Egypt, and Kenya. In 2019, investors from these countries who visited Thailand ranged from 1,365 to 4,718 persons. South Africa is particularly keen to establish a trade partnership with Thailand. As early as 1995, two years after the establishment of diplomatic ties with Thailand, the South African-Thai Chamber of Commerce was founded. Yet, it is noteworthy that those investors are mainly white South Africans (i.e., 'good guys') and, consequently, do not need to overcome Thai prejudice about Black Africans (Frontani 2015).

African gems traders are welcomed in Thailand, up to a point. They bring raw precious stones from Africa to be cut and sold in Thailand. Sapphires and rubies, mainly from Madagascar and Mozambique, have been exported to Chanthaburi, one of the biggest gem markets in Thailand (Vungsiriphisal, this volume; Chowdhury & Abid 2018). Thai traders also travel to Africa to purchase rubies in Mozambique. In the mid-1990s, there were 200–300 Thai gem traders living in Mozambique (Duggleby 2014), while 700 Africans lived in Chanthaburi in 2018. The African traders come from Cameroon, Côte d'Ivoire, Gambia, Ghana, Kenya, Madagascar, Mali, Nigeria, Kenya, Sierra Leone, and Zambia.

Other Africans engage in circular migration to purchase inexpensive products in Thailand for resale in Africa. Designer-knockoff clothes and shoes produced in Thailand are particularly popular with African women (Friedman 2015). Women from Sub-Saharan and West Africa are the major traders of budget clothes, shoes, and hair/beauty products. Pratunam Market in Bangkok remains popular among African traders (Unor & Thabchumpon, this volume).

Most African traders come to Thailand on tourist visas, which allow them to stay for 90 days. The West African traders, dominated by Nigerians, buy clothes, shoes, and cosmetics in Bangkok. Africans are also involved in logistics; they pack products in containers and ship them to West Africa. It is difficult to estimate the number of these traders (Ukam Unor & Thabchumpon, this volume).

The 'good guys' also include professionals (mainly English language teachers) and athletes (mainly footballers). Growing numbers of foreign-born English speakers from the Global South are migrating to Thailand to seek work as English teachers (Hickey 2018). While English speakers from African countries are coveted by Thai private schools, the Black Africans are disadvantaged where 'whiteness' signifies aspirations of global mobility and transnational cosmopolitanism (Ruecker & Ives 2015). Finding work in Bangkok and desirable housing is especially difficult for African English teachers, so many decide to apply directly to schools in smaller cities and rural areas (Hickey 2018).

Another group of Africans who come to Thailand are professional athletes. In the 1990s, Thailand recruited Africans to play soccer in major football clubs (Romero & Thammasaengadipha, this volume) because of their strength and endurance (Interview, Football Club manager, Bangkok, July 17, 2019). In 2014, a new regulation from the Immigration Bureau prevented foreign professional athletes, including Africans, from coming to Thailand on tourist visas looking for employment in sports. Only high-level clubs or sports associations could apply for athlete visas for professionals. As of 2021, fewer African athletes are employed in Thailand but, nevertheless, are considered 'good guys' by immigration police.

Foreign-born students seek higher education in Thailand. Two decades ago, there were fewer than 2,000 African students in Thailand. Today, the country is the third-most popular destination for African students in Southeast Asia, after Malaysia and Singapore. Currently, Thailand hosts some 30,000 foreign students of all nationalities. Thai universities now offer over 1,000 international programs in English, and the number registered in joint degree programs – which involve studying for two years in Thailand and two years abroad – more than doubled between 2012 and 2015 (Seneviratne 2018; Chaiyasat 2020).

Many Asian governments have initiated a South–South cooperation policy by granting scholarships to African students to study in Asia. These scholarships are significant elements for *Bridging the Best of Asia and Africa* (Asiafrica Foundation n.d.). Between 2008 and 2015, TICA provided 112 scholarships and 1,667 training fellowships to African students.

Some African students enter Thailand on a student visa issued on the basis of enrollment in a local university. These students depend on financial assistance from their own social networks although the universities usually offer scholarships to cover 50 percent of full tuition (Kiarie, this volume).

## *'Bad guys:'* Drug dealers and other criminals

Like other foreign nationals, Africans come to Thailand to study, work, or explore other pursuits. Those who bring the country economic benefit are welcomed. However, those who come as tourists, especially Black Africans, may be considered prone to criminal activity based on racial profiling by Thai immigration officers, the police, and even society at large, and less desirable.

As noted, Thais are less familiar with Black Africans than other groups of people. Many Thais may base their negative opinion of Black Africans on sensationalized news coverage of arrests on drug charges, fraud, or other criminal offenses by foreigners, but linking Black people with drug use goes back to the Vietnam War when some American GIs allegedly engaged in drug abuse and prostitution. American soldiers, both White and Black, used drugs heavily during the Vietnam War (Janos 2018). Some GIs married Thai bar girls (Davies 2005). The use of drugs and affiliation with sex workers have resulted in linking Black people with drugs and prostitution.

In the 1990s and 2000s, Thailand became an important transit point for drug trafficking in Southeast and East Asia (Windle 2016). A growing number of native Thai and foreign drug traffickers were involved in the drug trade (WHO 2010). The Thai Office of Narcotics Control Board (ONCB) indicated that Africans participated in this trade. Reportedly, West African gangs trafficked cocaine and methamphetamines through international airports into Thailand (AIPA 2019).

The *Bangkok Post* reported since 2011 that some Africans used Thai women as drug mules to transport drugs internationally (Fernquest 2011). Some bribed African women to carry narcotics in their dreadlocks (Grobler 2019). In October 2014, Thai police arrested three African men on charges of possession of crystal methamphetamine with intent to sell (Bangkok Post 2014). Recent reports provide further examples of the involvement of Africans in the drug trade. In 2019, a Kenyan and a Nigerian drug smuggler were arrested at the airport when X-rays revealed they carried drugs in their stomachs. The ONCB later exchanged information about transnational drug networks with Japanese police and customs officials. The cooperation had led to the arrest of people behind the smuggling, mostly members of African drug networks (Laohong 2019). In 2020, a large drug deal operation called *Black Sashimi* was intercepted at the Bangkok airport. *Black Sashimi* was a network of Nigerians in Thailand who sent methamphetamine to counterparts in Japan (Udon News 2020). It is noteworthy that dark-skinned individuals are also racially profiled by Thai immigration police even when they are not engaged in drug trafficking.

In reality, the number of Africans arrested on drug smuggling charges is relatively small in comparison to other groups of migrants. However, the media and police reports have created a negative perception, both among Thai authorities and the general public, and Black Africans continue to be stigmatized as drug dealers (Unor, this volume). A representative of the ONCB indicated that male West African drug dealers use fraudulent travel documents and entice Thai women to open a bank account, rent apartments, and even marry them in order to obtain long-term visas or to help traffic drugs. Between 1989 and 2002, an average of 30–50 cases a year of West Africans dealing in drugs in Thailand was reported. The police arrested 172 Africans on charges of drug possession in 2001 and Nigerians were most frequently arrested (Chavalit & Permpong 2016).

In 2001, the Ministry of Interior raised concerns over fraudulent marriages between African men and Thai women. The Ministry discovered that these 'marriages of convenience' were used to entice Thai women to carry drugs to international destinations. Countries with a significant number of male marriage scammers with Thai women are Nigeria, Ghana, and the Ivory Coast (Chuenniran 2020; O'Conner 2019). In 2014, the Secretary of the Council of State annulled many of these marriages (Office of the Council of State 2014).

## Conclusions

The number of migrants from Africa in Thailand is small but growing. However, despite the small size of the African community, the presence of Black migrants causes anxiety among Thai authorities and the general public. We argue that some of this anxiety is related to ignorance about Africa and Africans and lack of meaningful contacts with Africans residing in Thailand. The police mainly interface with criminals, and the news media publish sensationalistic articles about the 'bad guys' arrested on criminal or immigration violations. These kinds of reports shape the perceptions of Thais about Africans. Human interest stories about the 'good guys' from Africa are rare.

Thai immigration policy does not overtly discriminate against Africans. However, Thai immigration authorities scrutinize visa applications from Africans more closely and view Africans entering on tourist visas with suspicion, assuming that once they enter Thailand they would stay illegally and engage in criminal activities. Also, lack of familiarity with Black Africans leads to stereotypes and fear in contrast to more frequent contact with Caucasians who come to Thailand in greater numbers as tourists, business people, or long-term residents.

We posit, however, that Thai fear of Africans is not structurally embedded in society at large. Rather, this bias might be fomented by the police. Furthermore, the concern among Thais is a wariness, not hatred or racism *per se*. Following Appadurai (2006), we argue that discrimination against Black Africans resembles discrimination of the lower castes in India. Pravit Rojanaphruk (2020) considers the term 'cultural chauvinism' as more accurate than racism, at least the American version of racism, which he links to slavery.

We also see similarities between the Thai perception of African migrants and attitudes toward low-skill migrant workers employed in jobs which Thais shun as being undignified (Chintayanonda et al. 1997). According to surveys conducted by ILO and UN Women, the vast majority (77 percent) of Thais thought that the crime rate had increased due to migration, and 58 percent thought that migrant workers could not be trusted. The authors of the study concluded that the public has limited knowledge about migrant workers, resulting in negative attitudes and lack of support (ILO 2019).

A paradigm shift in Thai attitudes toward African migrants might take some time. Such a change would have to start with education at a young age under the theme of 'skillful living in a globalized world.' The Ministry of Foreign Affairs (MOFA) could help promote better understanding of Africa and its people. In 2017 and 2019, the MOFA and African Embassies in Bangkok organized *Colors of Africa* festivals to promote cultural exchange and awareness of trade and investment opportunities in Africa (Muqbil 2019).

Before the paradigm shift is realized, Thailand should develop a more coherent immigration policy to accommodate the diverse groups of migrants who are interested in coming to Thailand. More bilateral agreements for visa exemptions with African countries should be considered. The visa extension processes should be seamless and should not arbitrarily disadvantage Black Africans. Thai consulates/embassies in African countries should be more active in educating people about travel to Thailand. African migrants should be treated as any other migrant.

Asylum procedures must meet international standards, including screening of asylum applications, refugee status determination (RSD), and protection of *bona fide* refugees. There should be support for asylum seekers/refugees as they await the adjudication of their cases and/or resettlement in third countries. Active coordination between the Thai Immigration Bureau, UNHCR, and civil society organizations is required to better assist asylum seekers.

Arresting African refugees already screened by UNHCR and detaining them in the Immigration Detention Center (IDC) together with illegal immigrants is a violation of their rights and must be stopped. The Ministerial Regulation on the Screening of Aliens Entering Thailand who Cannot Return to Place of Origin (2019) must be strictly implemented in close consultation with UNHCR. With reference to the 1998 South African Refugee Act on how South Africa is dealing with urban refugees, Thailand should consider setting up shelters in Bangkok to host African refugees. The shelters should separate urban refugees from illegal immigrants detained in the IDC, provide them with humanitarian protection, and facilitate resettlement.

# References

AIPA. (2019). 'Thailand Country Report. Report of the Second Meeting of the AIPA Advisory Council on Dangerous Drugs,' Available at: https://www.parliament.go.th/ewtadmin/ewt/aipa2019/download/article/AIPACODD/1_Report.pdf

Alastair, G. M. (2018). 'Bangkok's Somali Refugees Persecuted and Living in Fear,' *Aljazeera*, 20 January. Available at: https://www.aljazeera.com/features/2018/1/20/bangkoks-somali-refugees-persecuted-and-living-in-fear

Appadurai, Arjun. (2006). *Fear of Small Numbers: An Essay on the Geography of Anger*. Durham: Duke University Press.

Asiafrica Foundation. (n.d.). *Bridging the Best of Asia and Africa*. Available at: https://www.asiafricafoundation.org/

Bangkok Post Reporters. (2014). 'Africans Arrested on Drug Charges,' *Bangkok Post*, 30 October. Available at: https://www.bangkokpost.com/thailand/general /440465/africans-arrested-for-drug-charges

Bruton, Christopher. (2019). 'Thailand Immigration Controls: Getting Tough with Guests,' *Bangkok Post*, 24 June. Available at: https://www.bangkokpost.com/ business/1700888/thailand-immigration-controls-getting-tough-with-guests

Chaiyasat, Chatchawan. (2020). 'Overseas Students in Thailand: A Qualitative Study of Cross-Cultural Adjustment of French Exchange Students in a Thai University Context,' *Journal of Human Behavior in the Social Environment*, 30 (8), pp. 1060–1081. doi: 10.1080/10911359.2020.1792386

Chantavanich, Supang. (1999). 'Thailand's Responses to Transnational Migration during Economic Growth and Economic Downturn,' *Sojourn: Journal of Social Issues in Southeast Asia*, 14 (1), pp. 159–177.

Chantavanich, Supang. (2011). 'Cross-Border Displaced Persons from Myanmar in Thailand,' in Huguet, Jerrold W. & Chamratrithirong, Apichart (eds), *Thailand Migration Report 2011*, pp. 117–129. Bangkok: International Organization for Migration.

Chantavanich, Supang. (2020). 'Thailand's Challenges in Implementing Anti-Trafficking Legislation: The Case of the Rohingya,' *Journal of Human Trafficking*, 6 (2), pp. 34–243.

Chantavanich, Supang & Reynolds, Bruce E. (eds). (1988). *Indochinese Refugees: Asylum and Resettlement*. Bangkok: Institute of Asian Studies, Chulalongkorn University.

Chavalit, Permpong. (2016). 'Drug trafficking among West Africans in Thailand,' in Reunkaew, Pattaya, Chantavanich, Supang, & Wungeo, Chantana (eds), *Emigration and Immigration in Thailand: Sociology of Transnational Lives* (in Thai), pp. 257–284. Bangkok: Chulalongkorn University Press.

Chintayananda, Sudthichitt, Risser, Gary, & Chantavanich, Supang. (1997). *Report on the Monitoring of the Registration of Immigrant Workers from Myanmar, Cambodia and Laos in Thailand*. Bangkok: Asian Research Center for Migration, Institute of Asian Studies, Chulalongkorn University.

Chowdhury, Arnab Roy & Abid, Ahmed. (2018). 'Hill of Gems, Gems of Labor – Mining in the Borderlands,' *Kyoto Review of Southeast Asia*, 29.

Chuenniran, Achadthaya. (2020). '2 Nigerians Arrested Over Romance Scam,' *The Bangkok Post*, 13 September. Available at: www.bangkokpost.com/thailand/ general/1984567/2-nigerians-arrested-over-romance-scam

Colbey, Adele. (2018). 'Arbitrary Arrests Make Life in Bangkok Hell for African Migrants,' *Prachatai English*, 20 June. Available at: https://prachatai.com/ english/node/7773

Daily News. (2017). 'Massive Raid as "Coloreds" Targeted in Nana this Morning,' *The Nation News*, 16 September. Available at: https://forum.thaivisa.com/topic /1002502-massive-raid-as-coloreds-targeted-in-nana-this-morning/

Davies, Hugh. (2005). 'Wild Days of R&R in Vietnam,' *The Telegraph*, 26 March. Available at: https://www.telegraph.co.uk/news/worldnews/northamerica/usa/1486503/Those-wild-days-of-R-and-R-in-Vietnam.html

Dewansyah, Bilal & Handayani, Irawati. (2018). 'Reconciling Refugee Protection and Sovereignty in ASEAN Member States: Law and Policy Related to Refugee in Indonesia, Malaysia and Thailand,' *Central European Journal of International and Security Studies*, 12 (4), pp. 473–485.

Duggleby, Luke. (2014). 'Tricks and Stones: The Gem Traders of Chanthaburi,' *Post Magazine*, 10 August. Available at: https://www.scmp.com/magazines/post-magazine/article/1569045/tricks-and-stones

Fernquest, Jon. (2011). 'African Drug Gangs Target Thai Women,' *Bangkok Post*, 14 February. Available at: https://www.bangkokpost.com/learning/advanced/221542/african-drug-gangs-target-thai-women

Friedman, Hazel. (2015). 'Hope Dwindles for Women Imprisoned in Thailand for Drug Trafficking,' *Mail and Guardian*, 29 October. Available at: https://mg.co.za/article/2015-10-29-hope-dwindles-for-women-imprisoned-in-thailand-for-drug-trafficking/

Frontani, Heidi G. (2015). 'Success Story from Uganda: Andrew Rugasira's Good African Coffee,' *African Development Success blog*. https://africandevelopmentsuccesses.wordpress.com/2015/01/31/success-story-from-uganda-andrew-rugasiras-good-african-coffee/

Goździak, Elżbieta M. (2021). *Human Trafficking as a New (In)Security Threat*. Cham: Palgrave Macmillan.

Goździak, Elżbieta M., Main, Izabella, & Suter, Brigitte. (2020). *Europe and the Refugee Response a Crisis of Values?* London: Routledge.

Grimwade, Mary & Neumann, Petra. (2019). 'Migration Policy and Practice in Thailand,' in Harkins, Ben (ed), *Thailand Migration Report 2019*. Bangkok: International Organization for Migration.

Grobler, Riaan. (2019). 'Drug Mule Caught with Cocaine in Dreadlocks Returns to SA on Thursday,' *News24*, 19 September. Available at: https://www.news24.com/SouthAfrica/News/drug-mule-caught-with-cocaine-in-dreadlocks-returns-to-sa-on-thursday-20190919

Hall, Andy. (2011). 'Migration and Thailand: Policy, Perspectives and Challenges,' in Huguet, Jerrold W. & Chamratrithirong, Aphichat (eds), *Thailand Migration Report 2011*, pp. 17–38. Bangkok: International Organization for Migration.

Haugen Østbø, Heidi. (2018). 'From Pioneers to Professionals: African Brokers in a Maturing Chinese Marketplace,' *African Studies Quarterly*, 17 (4), pp. 45–62.

Hickey, Maureen. (2018). 'Thailand's 'English Fever,' Migrant Teachers and Cosmopolitan Aspirations in an Interconnected Asia,' *Discourse: Studies in the Cultural Politics of Education*, 39 (5), pp. 738–751. doi: 10.1080/01596306.2018.1435603

Hua Hin Today. (2016). 'Good Guys in, Bad Guys out,' Says Thailand Immigration Chief,' *Hua Hin Today*, 1 February. Available at: https://www.huahintoday.com/sports/good-guys-in-bad-guys-out-says-thailand-immigration-chief/

Human Rights Watch. (2017). *Thailand: Implement Commitments to Protect Refugee Rights, End Detention, Forcible Returns of Refugees.* New York: Human Rights Watch.

ILO. (2019). 'Public Attitudes Towards Migrant Workers Remain Unfavorable in ASEAN Destination Countries,' Available at: http://www.ilo.org/asia/media -centre/news/WCMS_732449/lang--en/index.htm

Immigration Bureau. (2020a). *Immigration History.* Available at: https://www .immigration.go.th/en/?page_id=1396

Immigration Bureau. (2020b). *Permanent Residence Book.* Available at: https:// www.immigration.go.th/en/?page_id=2464

Immigration Statistics. (2020). *Statistics of the People Traveling in-out Thailand 2015–2018.* Available at: https://www.immigration.go.th/?page_id=1564

Janos, Adam. (2018). 'Drugs in the Vietnam War,' Available at: https://www.arcgis .com/apps/Cascade/index.htmlappid=b59fef8b2af345d28553d58509b365a2

Jones, Catherine. (2015). 'Indonesia, Malaysia and Thailand Still Aren't Taking Real Responsibility for Refugees,' Blog post. https://theconversation.com/indonesia -malaysia-and-thailand-still-arent-taking-real-responsibility-for-refugees-42140

Kerwin, Donald. (2016). 'How Robust Refugee Protection Policies Can Strengthen Human and National Security,' *Journal of Migration and Human Security*, 4 (3), pp. 83–140.

Lang, Hazel. (2001). 'The Repatriation Predicament of Burmese Refugees in Thailand: A Preliminary Analysis,' *New Issues in Refugee Research Working Paper 46.* Available at: https://www.refworld.org/pdfid/4ff5661a2.pd

Laohong, King-Oua. (2019). 'Kenyan Had 1.2 kg of Cocaine in his Stomach,' *Bangkok Post*, 21 August. Available at: https://www.bangkokpost.com/thailand/ general/1734319/kenyan-had-1-2kg-of-cocaine-in-his-stomach

Ministry of Foreign Affairs. (2019). *Thailand Visa Types.* Available at: https://www .mfa.go.th/en/page/types-of-visa?menu=5e1ff6d757b01e00965d1682

Mokkhasen, Sasiwan. (2016). 'Police Put Calm Face on Raids Throughout Capital,' *Khaosod English*, 11 October. Available at: https://www.khaosodenglish.com/ politics/2016/10/11/police-put-calm-face-raids-throughout-capital-video/

Muqbil, Imtiaz. (2019). 'Colors of Africa Festival Held in Bangkok to Drive Tourism, Trade,' *Travel Impact Newswire*, 9 September. Available at: https:// www.travel-impact-newswire.com/2019/09/colours-of-africa-festival-held-in -bangkok-to-drive-tourism-trade/

National Police Office. (2019). Order for the Restructuring of Immigration Divisions: Regulations on the Role and Responsibility of Divisions in the Immigration Bureau. Internal document (in Thai).

Ngamkham, Wassayos. (2017). 'Drugs Police Raid Shop Owned by Celeb's Husband,' *Bangkok Post*, 2 February. Available at: https://www.bangkokpost .com/thailand/general/1191360/drugs-police-raid-shop-owned-by-celebs -husband

O'Connor, Joseph. (2019). 'Online Scammers are an Organized Crime Group in Thailand Working with International Hackers,' *Thai Examiner.com*, 21 October. Available at: https://www.thaiexaminer.com/thai-news-foreigners/2019/10/21/ online-scammers-thailand-thai-women-people-facebook-money/

OECD/ILO. (2017). 'How Immigrants Contribute to Thailand's Economy,' in *OECD Development Pathways*. Paris: OECD Publishing.

Office of the Council of State. (2014). 'Note on the Annulation of Marriage Certificate Annulment Resulting from Family Registration Misconduct,' Available at: http://web.krisdika.go.th/data/comment/comment2/2557/c2_1311 _2557.htm

Panprom, Apichaya. (2020). *The Problems of the Repatriation of Detainees under the Control of the Immigration Detention Center, Sub Division 3*, Crime Investigation Division, Immigration Bureau (Master's thesis). Bangkok: Chulalongkorn University.

Park, Min Jee Yamada. (2020). 'Thailand's National Screening Mechanism Paves the Way for Better Refugee Protection,' *ReliefWeb*, 7 February. Available at: https://reliefweb.int/report/thailand/thailand-s-national-screening-mechanism -paves-way-better-refugee-protection

Pongsapich, Amara & Chongwatana, Noppawan. (1988). 'The Refugee Situation in Thailand,' in Chantavanich, Supang & Reynolds, Bruce (eds), *Indochinese Refugees: Asylum and Resettlement*. Bangkok: Institute of Asian Studies, Chulalongkorn University.

Prachatai. (2019). 'Land of Smiles? Thailand's History of Deporting Refugees and Asylum Seekers,' *Prachatai*, 14 February. Available at: https://prachatai.com/ english/node/7929

Quinley, Caleb. (2019). 'Life in the Shadows: Thailand's Urban Refugees,' *New Humanitarian*, 11 September. Available at: https://www.thenewhumanitarian .org/news/2019/09/11/Thailand-refugee-policies-asylum-seekers-immigration -detention

Ruecker, Todd & Ives, Lindsay. (2015). 'White Native English Speakers Needed: The Rhetorical Construction of Privilege in Online Teacher Recruitment Spaces,' *TESOL Quarterly*, 49 (4), pp. 733–756P.

Rojanaphruk, Pravit. (2020). 'Opinion: From American Racism to Thai Chauvinism,' *Khaosod News*, 7 June. Available at: https://www.khaosodenglish.com/opinion /2020/06/07/opinion-from-american-racism-to-thai-chauvinism/

Saksornchai, Jintamas. (2018). 'Police Raid Khaosan, Nana in National Sweep of Foreigners,' *Khaosod English*, 19 April. Available at: https://www .khaosodenglish.com/news/bangkok/2018/04/19/police-raid-khaosan-nana-in -national-sweep-of-foreigners/

Seneviratne, Kalinga. (2018). 'International Programs Proliferate at Universities,' *University World News*, 16 November.

Severson, Adam. (2020). 'Thailand's Changing of the Guard: Negotiating the Transition from UNHCR Refugee Status Determination to a National Refugee Screening Mechanism,' *Refugee Law Initiative* Blog post. Available at: https:// rli.blogs.sas.ac.uk/2020/11/19/thailands-changing-of-the-guard-negotiating -the-transition-from-unhcr-refugee-status-determination-to-a-national-refugee -screening-mechanism/

Son, Johanna. (2018). 'For Urban Asylum Seekers, Uncertainty is the Certainty,' *Bangkok Post*, 28 May. Available at: https://www.bangkokpost.com/opinion/opinion/1474153/for-urban-asylum-seekers-uncertainty-is-the-certainty

Sucharitkul, Sompong. (1990). 'Thai Nationality in International Perspective,' *Publications*, 670. Available at: http://digitalcommons.law.ggu.edu/pubs/670

Tarrosy, Istvan. (2018). 'Thailand's Engagement with Africa. Yet Another "Unusual Suspect" is Intensifying Relations with African Countries. How Far Can It Go?,' *The Diplomat*, 28 February. Available at: https://thediplomat.com/2018/03/thailands-engagement-with-africa/

Thailand Alien Employment Permit Act. (1978). *Government Gazette*, 95 (73).

Thailand Embassy in Pretoria. 2019. 'Factsheet on South African Visitors to Thailand,' Unpublished document.

Thailand Immigration Act B.E.2522. (1979). *Royal Gazette*, 96 (28), p. 45. Available at: http://web.krisdika.go.th/data/outsitedata/outsite21/file/Immigration_Act_B.E._2522.pdf

Thailand Investment Promotion Act B.E.2520. (1977). Available at: http://web.krisdika.go.th

The Nation. (2016). 'Big Shortage of Qualified Technical and Skilled Workers,' *The Nation*, 4 November. Available at: https://www.nationthailand.com/national/30299195

Udon News. (2020). 'A Good Week at the Office for Narcotic Officers Shutting Down 4 Major Drug Networks,' *Udon News*, 10 June. Available at https://udon.info/2020/06/10/a-good-week-at-the-office-for-narcotic-officers-shutting-down-4-major-drug-networks/

UNHCR. (2000). *The State of the World's Refugees 2000 Chapter 4: Flight from Indochina*. Available at: https://www.unhcr.org/publications/sowr/4a4c754a9/state-worlds-refugees-2000-fifty-years-humanitarian-action.html

Vungsiriphisal, Premjai, Chusri, Dares, & Chantavanich, Supang (eds.). (2014). 'Humanitarian Assistance for Displaced Persons from Myanmar,' *Springer Briefs in Environment, Security, Development and Peace*, 17 (4), pp. 14–20.

WHO. (2010). *A Strategy to Halt and Reverse the HIV Epidemic Among People Who Inject Drugs in Asia and the Pacific: 2010–2015*. Available at: http://www.unodc.org/documents/southeastasiaandpacific/2010/07/hivstrategy/Harm_Reduction_Strategy_Asia_Pacific

Windle, James. 2016. *Drugs and Drug Policy in Thailand*. Washington, DC: Brookings Institute. https://www.brookings.edu/wp-content/uploads/2016/07/WindleThailand-final.pdf

World Integrated Trade Solution. (2019). *Thailand Trade Balance, Exports and Imports by Country and Region 2019*. Available at: https://wits.worldbank.org/CountryProfile/en/Country/THA/Year/2019/TradeFlow/EXPIMP/Partner/all#

Yeoh, Brenda. (2006). 'Bifurcated Labor: The Unequal Incorporation of Transmigrants in Singapore,' *Tijdschrift voor Economische en Sociale Geografie*, 97 (1), pp. 26–37. doi: 10.1111/j.1467-9663.2006.00493.x

# 4 Somali asylum seekers in Bangkok

## Coping strategies of the (in)visible and (in)secure

*Fatma Issa*

## Introduction

Bangkok is a city of over 10 million people. It is easy to be invisible in this huge metropolis unless one is an African. Despite small numbers, Africans are physically very visible in a city that has few Black people hailing from the African continent, while remaining socially invisible due to their undocumented status and discrimination.

Migration from Africa to Thailand is a recent phenomenon. Researchers from the Institute for Population and Social Research at Mahidol University estimate that approximately 8,100 Africans lived in Bangkok in 2017 (Vapattanawong 2017). This is a significant increase from the count provided by the 2010 Census that put the number of Africans in Bangkok at 3,000.

Africans come to Bangkok for a variety of reasons. Magan,[1] a 23-year-old Somali man fled Somalia after his family was killed. He said: 'It took me almost one year before I could stop crying every time, I remembered that day.' Beydan, a young Somali woman, told me she was persecuted because she married a man from a lower social class and clan. When her husband and two of his brothers were killed by local militia, she fled Somalia.

Three of my female interlocutors indicated that they had to flee due to pressure to donate their kidneys. One of the women explained that after the death of her parents, she was adopted by the family that her mother worked for as a housekeeper. Aamiina was not aware that her foster family planned to sell her kidney until the foster mother had taken her to a hospital for 'checkups.'

Several of the interviewed women were victims of gender-based violence. Abused by their husbands, they had no one to turn to for help as the community turned a blind eye to the physical and mental abuse they endured. Having lost their families and being married off at a very young

DOI: 10.4324/9781003286554-4

age, they felt they had no other option, but to leave. They believed that to the community they left behind they are considered shameless and disgraceful.

In some instances, the migrants fell prey to 'agents' who advertised their services to bring Somalis to Thailand where life is supposedly cheaper and better. However, once people arrived in Bangkok, the 'agent' had no job prospects and often left them to their own devices.

Most of my interlocutors, especially the women, had never traveled outside Somalia and had very limited understanding of world geography. Some were under the impression that they were going to Europe because they heard rumors that the agent they were working with 'had connections in Europe.' Mariam, a single mother, recalled how her 'agent' took total control of her trip. She did not know she was destined to travel to Thailand and had no idea how long her trip would take. She ended up in Bangkok with her son in tow, a small backpack, and $300.

Although a few people traveled through Dubai, most were flown to Malaysia, where they stayed for a few hours or a few days. From Kuala Lumpur they were transported, illegally, by bus to Thailand. In some cases, the agents took the passports of their charges; some of the women did not understand how important passports are for international travel. While they agreed to leave Somalia, and paid the smugglers, in certain cases their experiences resembled human trafficking.

No matter who they are and why they came to Bangkok, the Somalis have few options in Thailand. Thailand is not a signatory of the 1951 Refugee Convention nor the 1967 Protocol relating to the Status of Refugees; therefore, there is no possibility to acquire refugee status or gain asylum in the country. However, the presence of the United Nations High Commissioner for Refugees (UNHCR) in Bangkok provides some refugees with the hope that they might register with the UN Refugee Agency to gain a certain level of protection and apply to be recognized as *bona fide* refugees in order to be resettled in North America, Australia, or Europe.

Lenient visa requirements allow Africans with appropriate resources to enter Thailand as tourists. Those who engage in trade use tourist visas to enable their transcontinental entrepreneurial activities. However, those who overstay their tourist visas quickly become undocumented and need to make themselves invisible to the immigration authorities. Most of the people I encountered during my research live in the shadows trying to avoid encounters with law enforcement and immigration authorities.

Using data from an exploratory study with several Somalis residing in Bangkok, I interrogate the interplay of visibility and invisibility within the context of human (in)security. I present narratives from Somali men and women to unpack their coping strategies to remain physically invisible to authorities while trying to secure a degree of economic security. I also present data from interviews with civil society organizations assisting Somalis in their pursuit of legal remedies to come out of the shadows and lead their lives with dignity.

Africans are part of the 5,000 urban refugees and asylum seekers representing 40 nationalities who live in Bangkok and the surrounding urban areas (UNHCR Thailand website). Urban refugees have received much attention in the migration literature. As early as 2006, the *Journal of Refugee Studies* published a special issue on urban refugees. In the editorial introduction, Karen Jacobsen (2006) emphasized that people displaced by armed conflict and the resulting destruction of livelihoods are increasingly likely to end up in large urban centers rather than in camps. The 2019 World Refugee Council report indicated that worldwide about 17.5 million (or 60 percent) of refugees live in urban areas (World Refugee Council 2019). In the early 2000s, only 18 percent of refugees lived in cities (Jacobsen 2006). As Cristiano D'Orsi (2019) argues, the increased number of urban refugees is a result of a conscious policy on the part of the UN Refugee Agency which recognizes that camps can easily turn into detention centers (UNHCR 2009). Additionally, the increased number of urban refugees stems from the fact that refugees do not like being housed in camps. On the other hand, argues D'Orsi (2019), host countries prefer camps because they can easily control refugees and can force the international community to take responsibility.

While UNHCR acknowledges that more and more refugees move into the cities, the UN Refugee Agency offers few recommendations on how cities could serve them better. In practice, that means that urban refugees mostly fend for themselves and receive little protection from UNHCR. *Forced Migration Review* (2010) dedicated its 34th issue to the challenges of protecting refugees and internally displaced persons (IDPs) living in large cities. In their introductory articles, UN High Commissioner for Refugees António Guterres (2010) and UN-HABITAT Executive Director Anna Tibaijuka (2010) emphasized the complexity of the challenges faced by those displaced in urban areas and by those seeking to protect and assist them, and argued for a radical rethinking of approaches by the international community.

The literature on urban refugees deals with refugees living in urban centers in South Africa, Egypt, Uganda, Pakistan, Colombia, and many other places (see Landau 2014). It includes some research on urban refugees in Bangkok. Palmgren (2014) examined informal networks of mobility, subsistence, and information utilized by Khmer Krom, Rohingya, and Vietnamese refugees and asylum seekers. He argued that through such networks, these displaced people are exercising forms of agency that allow for some navigation through Thailand's criminalizing immigration framework as well as

Southeast Asia's bleak refugee rights protection landscape. Thoresen et al. (2017) studied the needs of urban refugee and asylum-seeking children living in precarious circumstances in Bangkok. This study privileged the perspectives of children and compared them with those of adults: their parents and guardians as well as service providers and policy advocates.

None of the papers on urban refugees in Bangkok focus on African asylum seekers. Generally speaking, while there is a growing literature on African migrants in China (see Lan 2015a, b; McLaughlin et al. 2014; Bredeloup 2012; Lyons et al. 2012), there is very scarce research on Africans in Thailand. Gonah et al. (2016) examine access to healthcare and coping mechanisms among Sub-Saharan Africans living in Bangkok. In their paper on stranded migrants, Gois and Campbell (2013) briefly mention Africans stranded in Thailand. The majority of writings about Africans in Thailand are newspaper articles.

I begin with a brief discussion of theoretical frameworks used to analyze my findings. I focus mainly on the interplay of visibility and invisibility and the nexus of (in)visibility and human security, especially economic security. The main part of this chapter includes findings from my exploratory empirical research. I end the chapter with a call for more research at the intersection of (in)visibility and illegality as well as human security.

## Visibility and invisibility of Somalis in Bangkok

Being Black, Somalis are physically very visible in Bangkok. They have different phenotypical features than ethnic Thais, are taller than most Asians, and they dress differently. These features often make them self-conscious when they are in public spaces. Somali women's attire, the *guntiino*, a long stretch of cloth tied over the shoulder and draped around the waist, also attracts attention. Although the *guntiino* is traditionally made out of plain white fabric sometimes featuring decorative borders, many Somali women in Bangkok use *alindi*, a textile common in the Horn of Africa and some parts of North Africa or other locally available colorful cloth. Thais notice these differences in physical appearance and different clothing styles and frequently point fingers at Somalis to draw attention to their 'otherness.' Young Thai girls giggle when they see Somali women or men in the street.

Somalis' social visibility, defined here as the everyday practices of seeing and being seen, is registered in multiple ways. Three of the interviewed Somalis talked about being singled out due to their appearance and dark complexion when trying to rent an apartment. Mohamad, a 23-year-old male, and his friend were turned away by 20 different landlords, most of whom said: 'Somali, No!' My male interlocutors experienced similar prejudice while looking for jobs. They said that whenever they went to construction sites, they would be picked last once all the other, non-African migrant workers had been chosen.

Some Somali women decided to start wearing Western clothes to be less visible. Mariam recalled the smuggler who facilitated her journey from Mogadishu to Bangkok telling her how to dress to blend in. Adapting clothing is often used to obscure overt visibility based on skin color on the street and as a strategy to avoid police scrutiny. Sarah Willen (2007) showed how Liberian migrants living in Tel Aviv completely covered their bodies with long-sleeved clothing and hats so people in the street would not see their black skin.

Writing about Nigerians in London, Caroline Knowles indicated that even in this large multiracial city, Nigerians' visibility was registered 'in bodies, in clothing, in performances, in forms of commerce, inflows of money, in artifacts and buildings' (Knowles 2012: 652). She argues that visibility may be obscured or revealed, involving 'complex dynamics of seeing and being seen,' refracted through multiple prisms of surveillance, media, and visual navigation of landscapes (Knowles 2012: 653). This is definitely true about Somalis living in Bangkok. Remaining vigilant to the presence of police and immigration authorities keeps undocumented Somalis on high alert. They are ready to disappear down an alley at a moment's notice. Undocumented Somalis have devised numerous strategies of masking their visibility, including staying inside, creating disguises to avoid police scrutiny, and adopting clandestine techniques of counterfeiting documents.

Social visibility of migrants is a gendered process, with women often socially invisible for reasons of physical immobility in countries of origin (Baird 2014). In Somalia, many women are restricted from moving about without the consent of a male guardian. As a result, they either do not migrate or if they do migrate, they might be confined to the private sphere of the home and might not venture outside as much as male migrants do. Several of the females in my study said they try to stay inside as much as they can. Those who do not work outside the home, venture out only on market days to buy food for their families. Those who participate in vocational training programs or other organized activities travel in small groups.

On the other hand, refugee and immigrant women often become very visible in public and political discourses. Writing about Muslim immigrant women in the Netherlands, Halleh Ghorashi (2010) shows how the invisible Muslim women became very visible within the discourse on integration and social cohesion. This new visibility, embedded in certain assumptions about societal and cultural 'shortcomings' of Muslim women, has had enormously stigmatizing consequences. Stereotyping Muslim women as isolated and unemancipated has served as an othering component of the discourse rather than creating space for their voices and experiences.

The Thai government's reluctance to address immigration positively can be explained, at least partially, as incompatibility with the conceptualization of social cohesion held by the government and Thai society at large. In the Thai context, social cohesion is equated with nationality and citizenship and as such relates mainly to ethnic Thais (Traitongyoo 2008). Temporary labor workers are expected to return to their countries of origin when their contracts expire (Huguet et al. 2012); therefore, no provisions to facilitate their integration into Thai society are in place. Even though most of the labor migrants are Asian, they do not fit into the Thai hegemonic production of identity (Connors 2005).

Migrants are often considered invisible, voiceless, and marginalized populations. 'Sometimes this invisibility is favored by a commonality of language, customs, and religion, as between Indonesia and Malaysia. Sometimes their visibility is tolerated, as in Thailand, since they are functional to the local economy' (Battistellea 2017). While documented migrants strive for visibility and recognition, undocumented migrants want to become invisible, especially to immigration authorities.

Hiding from the police is not always easy in Bangkok as Thai authorities continue to target African migrants, citing a high incidence of criminal activities in the African diaspora communities. *Operation Black Eagle*, initiated in July 2017, on the orders of junta leader Prayut Chan-o-cha, was an attempt by the police to clamp down on African migrants committing crimes in Thailand. The leader of a raid during which more than 80 foreigners were detained, described it as specifically targeting Black people. The targeting of Africans drew criticism of the Thai police. However, Deputy Police Spokesperson Kritsana Pattanacharoen denied that *Operation Black Eagle* was racist. 'It's called Black Eagle, not black people,' he told Prachatai English, and added, 'it's not the only operation [the police] have been conducting; we have a lot of operations targeting illegal foreigners' (Colbey 2018).

This assertion is not shared by Africans living in Bangkok. Most feel they have been singled out among the foreign residents. Several of my interlocutors talked about police raids and arrests. Abshir said:

> I had been arrested one time before. Getting arrested is one of the things we are very afraid of as urban refugees. We hear stories about the detention center and we all don't want to end there. So, whenever anyone of us gets arrested, we usually give the police everything we have just so we don't go to the detention center. I am afraid I will not be lucky next time I am arrested.

Discrimination against Black people is not rare in Thailand and neither is prejudice against immigrants. Data from the *World Values Survey Wave*

*6 Racial Prejudice Index* indicates that Thailand ranked the lowest, that is, most prejudiced, out of 59 territories. Between 2007 and 2013 the percentage of Thai respondents who mentioned that they would not like to have immigrants as neighbors increased from 43.4 percent to 58.3 percent. Draper and colleagues discuss this prejudice also in the context of internal prejudice using examples of tensions between Buddhist Thais and Muslim Thai Malays in the South, historically constructed 'othering' of citizens of Myanmar, and Central Thais' perception of Lao Thais as culturally inferior (Draper et al. 2019). The demonization of racial Others in the service of an ultra-nationalist Thai government has been well documented (Winichakul 2000) as have been negative attitudes towards migrant workers. According to an International Labor Organization (ILO) study, 72 percent of Thai society believes that immigrants commit a high number of crimes; 60 percent say migrant workers have a poor work ethic, and 58 percent of the Thai public tends to believe that migrant workers threaten the country's culture and heritage (ILO 2019).

Somalis' (in)visibility follows a zigzag pattern (de Vries 2016). They make themselves visible to UNHCR in order to be screened and issued a refugee identity card, but this process also makes them visible to the Thai authorities (Battistellea 2017) from whom they want to hide. De Vries discusses this zigzag process as the 'politics of (in)visibility' wherein the government dictates subjectivities by first making refugees and immigrants irregular, illegal, and invisible. Migrants are criminalized and become subject to state securitization. If refugees obtain protective status from UNHCR, their existence makes them now visible and knowable to the public (de Vries 2016).

## Human (in)security

Somalis' (in)visibility in Thailand, exacerbated by racism, discrimination, and prejudice, does not bode well for their security, both physical and human. The Thai government often cites the need to protect national security as a reason for curtailing admission of refugees (and other migrants). The government conceptualizes national security rather narrowly as being synonymous with territorial integrity. In my opinion, attempts to protect state security and sovereignty have to go hand-in-hand with efforts to ensure human security of both hosts and newcomers. The concept of security needs to be broadened and needs to incorporate safety from such chronic threats such as hunger, disease, and repression as well as protection from sudden and hurtful disruptions of daily life (Edwards 2009). There needs to be a recognition of the existence of threats from both within and outside the state. I write this fully cognizant that the concept of human security has been contested (King & Murray 2001). However, switching 'the referent from the state to individuals and shifting the focus from military threats to the state to political, economic, environmental, and gender-based threats to individuals' (MacFarlane & Khong 2006: 237) can be beneficial when it is used as a vehicle to help garner resources and attention from policy-makers for unconventional security issues (Aradau 2004), including the well-being of refugees and asylum seekers who fled both national and human insecurity resulting from armed conflicts.

Currently, there are two major schools of thought on how to best practice human security: freedom from fear and freedom from want (Hanlon & Christie 2016). The first school limits the practice of human security to protect individuals from violent conflicts while recognizing that these violent threats are strongly associated with poverty and other forms of inequities. This approach focuses on emergency assistance, conflict prevention, conflict resolution, and peace-building. The second school advocates a more holistic approach and argues that the threat agenda should take a broader view, including threats such as hunger, disease, and natural disasters. In my view, both apply to Somali asylum seekers in Thailand. The well-founded fear of persecution based on clan membership or political opinion (see Kiarie, this volume) prompted Somalis to seek refuge in Thailand (and elsewhere in the world). However, since Thailand is not a signatory of the Refugee Convention, this first type of human security is not practiced. Neither is the second.

Considered undocumented migrants, Somalis in Bangkok lead very precarious lives with no access to legal employment. One of the interviewed service providers indicated that despite the no employment rule, some urban refugees and asylum seekers look for jobs as they need to support themselves. She indicated that Somali refugees who speak English can work as interpreters for local non-governmental organizations (NGOs) assisting urban refugees. Only two of the Somalis in my sample spoke passable English and one spoke very basic Thai. Inability to communicate in Thai further limited their employment opportunities. Service providers remarked that if Somalis spoke at least some Thai, they would be able to get work in restaurants. Without Thai, it is difficult to secure any form of employment.

Somali women tend to work in the informal sector as domestic workers. Some also work in Arab-owned hotels as cleaners or in African-owned restaurants. Often these jobs make women vulnerable to exploitation, including sexual exploitation. Men tend to work in construction or as porters. Both men and women resort to working in the cash economy. I have also heard of Somali women who work as housekeepers for medical tourists from Europe and North America who come to Thailand for medical treatment. Somali men sometimes assist Arabic-speaking businessmen in locating markets and potential customers.

These jobs are very precarious and do not guarantee a stable source of income. Additionally, working in the shadow economy refugees are vulnerable to exploitation by employers. They earn very low wages and are expected to work long hours.

Every Somali I interviewed shared a story of exploitation. Astur and two of her friends were once hired to help package locally made drinks. After putting in a long day, they were paid half the amount agreed upon before the job commenced. When they questioned the employer, he threatened to call the police fully knowing that they would be detained. In cases of labor exploitation or sexual harassment on the job, Somalis are defenseless; they have nowhere to report workplace abuses as they risk becoming visible to immigration authorities.

Those who manage to secure employment in the informal sector cannot rely on being paid on time. Several of my interlocutors told me that at times they went without pay for a week or longer. Others were not guaranteed work even when they were promised a job. Abdullahi said that he once reported at a construction site for several days in a row hoping to be hired as day laborer, but the work never materialized.

This precarious employment leads to extreme poverty and dependence on charity. Mariam, a single mother, explained that she mostly relies on the allowance she receives from attending NGO-provided English language classes. The allowance is minimal, but 'it is better than nothing,' she said. On the days when she doesn't have work, she has to beg her neighbors to share their food so she can feed her son. Some asylum seekers receive a modest stipend from UNHCR, but it does not cover much. Idil remarked:

> The prices keep getting higher. The price of cooking oil and the price of bread has increased during the time I have been living in Bangkok. But sadly, the allowance we get from UNHCR is the same amount after all this time. What can we do?

One of the interviewees mentioned that the Jesuit Refugee Services (JRS) provide cash assistance, especially to children under the age of 18. A JRS staff member explained:

> We assist asylum seekers based on an initial assessment by a case worker. We support single mothers, disabled asylum seekers, unaccompanied minors, the elderly, and people with serious health or mental health issues. The assistance can last anywhere from three to six

months. We also provide emergency assistance for housing and pregnancy-related expenses.

Most of the assistance provided by NGOs is limited to facilitating access to healthcare, education, vocational training, and legal aid. The latter is particularly important when asylum seekers get detained or arrested. Others depend on remittances sent by relatives living in the United States or Europe. A few people came to Thailand with some savings. However, without stable employment, these savings were depleted in a very short time. One of the Somali interpreters told me that he came to Bangkok with a couple of thousand dollars, but with no place to live and no prospects of income, he used the money to cover his living expenses and the savings diminished very quickly.

Despite these seemingly insurmountable challenges, Somali refugees and asylum seekers scrape a living in Bangkok. In the following section, I will look at the adaptive strategies they deploy to survive.

## Adaptive strategies

Writing about the adaptation of forced migrants, many scholars focus on their psychological well-being (Berry 1997; Ryan et al. 2008; Kuo 2014). While some of my interlocutors mentioned feeling down or sad, most were preoccupied with their inability to secure decent livelihoods. This is consistent with Maslow's hierarchy of needs (Maslow 1943) where the fundamental needs (food, water, safety) form the basis of the pyramid depicting the hierarchy and the need for self-actualization and transcendence crowns the top.

In keeping with Maslow's depiction of needs, I use the 'displaced livelihoods' (Jacobsen 2014) theory to discuss adaptive strategies deployed by Somali asylum seekers in Bangkok. Livelihoods, defined by Chambers and Conway (1992) as the means of gaining a living, can be equated with human security. Jacobsen argues that this framework is warranted because 'the pursuit of livelihoods by forced migrants is different from other migrants or those who are equally poor or discriminated against' (Jacobsen 2014: 99). She emphasizes three crucial differences that create particular livelihood difficulties.

First, forced migrants begin from a position of loss, including loss of assets, family and community, and often emotional and physical health. Indeed, many of the Somalis living in Bangkok have lost homes and whole families. While a few brought with them some savings, the majority fled Somalia with little else than the clothes on their backs. Miriam and her son came to Thailand with one backpack and very little money.

Second, forced migrants must re-establish their livelihoods and ensure at least minimal human security in a policy context that is often weighted against them. As already emphasized, Thailand is not a signatory of the Refugee Convention and provides neither humanitarian assistance to asylum seekers from Africa nor grants asylum seekers access to employment. Those who work are employed in the cash economy and live their lives in the shadows. Undocumented asylum seekers not only do not have access to decent livelihoods, they also fear for their physical safety in the context of ongoing immigration raids.

Third, while UNHCR and some NGOs provide limited humanitarian assistance, this support is restricted in terms of its size and eligibility, leaving many Somalis impoverished. The strategies which Somalis utilize to overcome poverty and disempowerment are of great interest both to migration scholars and policy-makers. Below I present some of these strategies as well as the resources – personal, material, social, and cultural – they either had or needed (Ryan et al. 2008).

Personal resources can be physical (health, mobility, energy, and physical attractiveness) or psychological (skills and personal traits, including problem-solving and social skills, self-esteem, optimism, self-efficacy, and hope) in nature. Material resources include money, property, means of transport, and personal possessions. Paid employment can also be seen as a material resource. Social resources refer to the beneficial aspects of personal relationships, including emotional, informational, and tangible support, as well as the sense of identity and belonging that integration in a social network brings. Cultural resources include linguistic skills, literacy, education, computer skills, and occupational skills.

In the Somali community in Bangkok, resources were very gendered. Most of the women had no or very limited education, some were illiterate, and many never worked outside the home. Their occupational skills were therefore virtually nonexistent. They countered this lack of resources with a great deal of resiliency and a lot of life skills.

Despite hardships and vulnerabilities, Somalis found ways to improve, somewhat, their livelihoods in Bangkok. Many pulled resources together and shared living spaces to save on rent. Sharing accommodations comes with its own problems, including overcrowding and gender-based violence. Most of the women I interviewed shared a room with three or four other women. They also shared food or contributed money to purchase food.

The negative impacts of discrimination can be minimized with in-group support from other Somalis. In-group support has frequently been reported as a protective factor for minorities (Safdar et al.2009). Somalis have a strong sense of community. Many live in the same neighborhood or even the same building. They support each other, especially at the beginning when newcomers are unfamiliar with the city. Several of the young women I interviewed were taken in by older Somali women when they first arrived in Bangkok. Aisha said: 'I am currently living with a Somali woman whose husband lives in Canada. She took me in a few months ago when I had to leave the room I was living in because my roommates were arrested.' Faduma is 50 years old; she is leaving for Canada in a few days to join her husband. 'I will have to find somewhere else to live, but like before, I believe I will find another place within the community, Insha'Allah.'

Living in a tight-knit community is helpful to those Somalis who lost their entire families during the armed conflict in Somalia. Being surrounded by people who understand the resulting trauma is therapeutic. Sharing information about available services is also beneficial.

Maintaining ties with the African Muslim community pays off as well. *Zakāt* (alms-giving), one of the five pillars of Islam, is the giving of 2.5 percent of one's possessions (surplus wealth) to charity, generally to the poor and needy. It is often compared to the system of tithing and alms, but it serves principally as the welfare contribution to poor and deprived Muslims. The impoverished African asylum seekers benefit from this religious custom. Mohammed mentioned that he had been remembered by his fellow Muslims who shared food with him during *iftar* or Eid celebrations. He believed that these small forms of generosity helped him in his life in the city.

Local Thai Muslims also employ African Muslims. Mohammed's friend who is a plumber often gets hired by members of the Thai Muslim community. He offers his services at a reduced rate and gets recommended to other customers, not only because of lower prices but also because of his excellent workmanship.

Somalis are also part of larger African networks in Bangkok located in areas such as Nana in Sukhumvit, Lat Phrao, and even the Pratunam market. Smugglers are very familiar with these neighborhoods and usually drop off their charges there in the hopes that Africans who have been living in Bangkok for some time would help newcomers. Several of my interlocutors mentioned looking for other Africans in these neighborhoods to ask for help. They were indeed offered temporary shelter and free food. Africans who have been in Bangkok for a very long time can afford to lend money to new arrivals.

As evidenced by the stories narrated by Somali asylum seekers in Thailand, it is obvious that they suffer a great deal of economic insecurity. The Thai government limits admissions of refugees and other migrants for the sake of its national security. As a result, asylum seekers have been criminalized as illegal migrants and have had no access to employment in the formal sector, leading to precarious livelihoods and food insecurity. Limited support from UNHCR and civil society groups, including local mosques, allows them to survive, as do community-based self-help strategies.

## Conclusions

Forced migrants arrive in Thailand having experienced many losses. They confront numerous challenges as they try to achieve a level of human security and pursue livelihoods. Social exclusion mechanisms, ranging from lack of appropriate policy response to asylum seekers to xenophobia and harassment on the street, limit their rights and abilities to pursue income-generating activities.

This chapter is based on a small exploratory study and as such merely signals some important themes that require further study. There is a need to study the link between social (in)visibility and undocumented migration. In order to develop more sophisticated understandings of undocumented migrant livelihoods and survival strategies, scholars, migrant advocates, and policy-makers need to understand how migrants adapt to urban space through social visibility and invisibility (Baird 2014).

This study has presented Somali refugees' and asylum seekers' perspectives on human (in)security. There is a need to augment this perspective with the views of policy-makers, including representatives of the Thai government. Little is known about the attitudes of the members of the Thai civil society towards newcomers fleeing armed conflicts. Integration, even if it is to be temporary, happens at the local level. We must gain a better understanding of the relationships between Africans and Thais that go beyond sensationalistic reporting about crimes the Africans allegedly commit and about immigration violations.

## Note

1  All names are pseudonyms.

## References

Ardau, Claudia. (2004). 'The Perverse Politics of Four-Letter Words: Risk and Pity in the Securitization of Human Trafficking,' *Millennium: Journal of International Studies*, 33 (2), pp. 251–77.

Baird, Theodore. (2014). 'The More You Look the Less You See: Visibility and invisibility of Sudanese migrants in Athens, Greece,' *Nordic Journal of Migration Research*, 4 (1), pp. 3–10. doi: 10.2478/njmr-2013-0008

Battistellea, Graziano. (2017). 'From Invisibility to Recognition: Reflections on the Conditions of Migrants in Our Society,' *Scalabrini Migration Center*. Keynote address delivered at Exodus V. Available at: https://cmsny.org/publications/invisibility-recognition/

Berry, John W. (1997). 'Immigration, Acculturation, and Adaptation,' *Applied Psychology: An International Review*, 46, pp. 5–68.

Bredeloup, Sylvie. (2012). 'African Trading Post in Guangzhou: Emergent or Recurrent Commercial Form?,' *African Diaspora*, 5 (1), pp. 27–50. doi: 10.1163/187254612X646206

Chambers, Robert & Conway, Gordon. (1992). 'Sustainable Rural Livelihoods: Practical Concepts for the 21st Century,' *Institute of Development Studies*, 296, pp. 127–30.

Colbey, Adele. (2018). 'Arbitrary Arrests Make Life in Bangkok Hell for African Migrants,' *Prachatai English*, 20 June. Available at: https://prachatai.com/english/node/7773

Connors, Michael Kelly. (2005). 'Hegemony and the Politics of Culture and Identity in Thailand,' *Critical Asian Studies*, 37 (4), pp. 523–51. doi: 10.1080/114672710500348414

De Vries, Leonie A. (2016). 'Politics of (In)visibility: Governance-resistance and the Constitution of Refugee Subjectivities in Malaysia,' *Review of International Studies*, 42 (5), pp. 876–94.

D'Orsi, Cristiano. (2019). 'Refugee Camps Versus Urban Refugees: What's Been Said – and Done,' *The Conversation*, 3 November. Available at: https://reliefweb.int/report/world/refugee-camps-versus-urban-refugees-what-s-been-said-and-done

Draper, John, Sobieszczyk, Teresa, Crumpton, Charles D., Lefferts, H. L., & Chachavalpongpun, Pavin. (2019). 'Racial "Othering" in Thailand: Quantitative Evidence, Causes, and Consequences,' *Nationalism and Ethnic Politics*, 25 (3), pp. 251–72.

Edwards, Alice. (2009). 'Human Security and the Rights of Refugees: Transcending Territorial and Disciplinary Borders,' *Michigan Journal of International Law*, 30 (3), pp. 763–807.

Ghorashi, Halleh. (2010). 'From absolute invisibility to extreme visibility: Emancipation trajectory of migrant women in the Netherlands,' *Feminist Review*, 94 (1), pp. 75–79.

Gois, William & Campbell, Karen. (2013). 'Stranded Migrants: A Call to Rethink the Current Labor Migration Paradigm,' *Migration and Development*, 2 (2), pp. 157–72. doi: 10.1080/21632324.2013.802126

Gonah, L., Corwin, A., January, J., Shamu, S., Nyati-Jokomo, Z., & van der Putten, M. (2016). 'Barriers to Healthcare Access and Coping Mechanisms among Sub-Saharan African Migrants Living in Bangkok, Thailand: A Qualitative Study,' *Medical Journal of Zambia*, 43 (4), pp. 238–46.

Guterres, António. (2010). 'Protection Challenges for Persons of Concern in Urban Settings,' *Forced Migration Review*, 34, pp. 8–9. Available at: https://www.fmreview.org/urban-displacement/guterres

Hanlon, Robert J. & Christie, Kenneth. (2016). *Freedom from Fear, Freedom from Want: An Introduction to Human Security*. Toronto: University of Toronto Press.

Huguet, Jerry, Chamratrithirong, Aphichat, & Natali, Claudia. (2012). *Thailand at a Crossroads: Challenges and Opportunities in Leveraging Migration for Development*. Available at: https://www.migrationpolicy.org/research/Thailand-Leveraging-Migration

ILO. (2019). *Public Attitudes Towards Migrant Workers in Japan, Malaysia, Singapore and Thailand*. Available at: https://www.ilo.org/asia/publications/WCMS_732443/lang--en/index.htm

Jacobsen, Karen. (2006). 'Refugees and Asylum Seekers in Urban Areas: A Livelihoods Perspective,' *Journal of Refugee Studies*, 19 (3), pp. 273–86.

Jacobsen, Karen. (2014). 'Livelihoods and Economics in Forced Migration,' in Edited by Elena Fiddian-Qasmiyeh, Gil Loescher, Katy Long, and Nando Sigona *The Handbook of Refugee and Forced Migration Studies*, pp. 99–111, Oxford: Oxford University Press.

King, Gary & Murray, Christopher. (2001). 'Rethinking Human Security,' *Political Science Quarterly*, 116 (4), pp. 585–610.

Knowles, Caroline. (2012). 'Nigerian London: Re-mapping Space and Ethnicity in Superdiverse Cities,' *Ethnic and Racial Studies*, 36 (4), pp. 651–99. doi: 10.1080/01419870.2012.678874.

Kuo, Ben C. H. (2014). 'Coping, Acculturation, and Psychological Adaptation Among Migrants: A Theoretical and Empirical Review and Synthesis of the Literature,' *Health Psychology and Behavioral Medicine*, 2 (1), pp. 16–33. doi: 10.1080/21642850.2013.843459

Lan, Shanshan. (2015a). 'Between Mobility and Immobility: Undocumented African Migrants Living in the Shadow of the Chinese State,' in Wang, Donggen, He, Shenjing (eds.), *Mobility, Sociability and Well-being of Urban Living*, pp. 3–21. Berlin: Springer Verlag.

Lan, Shanshan. (2015b). 'State Regulation of Undocumented African Migrants in China: A Multi-scalar Analysis,' *Journal of Asian and African Studies*, 50 (3), pp. 289–304. doi:10.1177/0021909614531903

Landau, Loren. (2014). 'Urban Refugees and IDPs,' in Elena Fiddian-Qasmiyeh et al. (eds), *The Oxford Handbook of Refugee and Forced Migration Studies*. New York: Oxford University Press.

Lyons, Michal, Brown, Alison, & Zhigang, Li. (2012). 'In the Dragon's Den: African Traders in Guangzhou,' *Journal of Ethnic and Migration Studies*, 38 (5), pp. 869–88. doi: 10.1080/1369183X.2012.668030

Macfarlane, Neil & Khong, Yuen Foong. (2006). *Human Security and the UN: A Critical History*. Bloomington: Indiana University Press.

Maslow, Abraham. (1943). 'A Theory of Human Motivation,' *Psychological Review*, 50 (4), pp. 370–96. doi:10.1037/h0054346

McLaughlin, Megan M., Lee, Margaret C., Hall, Brian J., Bulterys, Marc, Li Ling, Li, & Tucker, Joseph D. (2014). 'Improving Health Services for African Migrants in China: A Health Diplomacy Perspective,' *Global Public Health*, 9 (5), pp. 579–89. doi: 10.1080/17441692.2014.908935

Palmgren, Pei A. (2014). 'Irregular Networks: Bangkok Refugees in the City and Region,' *Journal of Refugee Studies*, 27 (1), pp. 21–41. doi:10.1093/jrs/fet004

Ryan, Dermot, Dooley, Barbara, & Benson, Ciaran. (2008). 'Theoretical Perspectives on Post-Migration Adaptation and Psychological Well-Being among Refugees: Towards a Resource-Based Model,' *Journal of Refugee Studies*, 21 (1), pp. 1–18.

Safdar, S., Struthers, W., & van Oudenhoven, J. P. (2009). 'Acculturation of Iranians in the United States, the United Kingdom, and the Netherlands: A Test of the Multidimensional Individual Difference Acculturation (MIDA) Model,' *Journal of Cross-Cultural Psychology*, 40 (3), pp. 468–91.

Tibaijuka, Anna. (2010). 'Adapting to Urban Displacement,' *Forced Migration Review*, 34, p. 4. Available at: https://www.fmreview.org/urban-displacement/ tibaijuka

Thoresen, Paradee, Fielding, Angela, Gillieatt, Sue, & Thoresen, Stian H. (2017). 'Identifying the Needs of Refugee and Asylum-Seeking Children in Thailand: A Focus on the Perspectives of Children,' *Journal of Refugee Studies*, 30 (3), pp. 426–46.

Traitongyoo, Krongkwan. (2008). *The Management of Irregular Migration in Thailand: Thainess, Identity and Citizenship* (Doctoral dissertation). Leeds: University of Leeds.

UNHCR. (2009). *UNHCR Policy on Refugee Protection and Solutions in Urban Areas*. Available at: https://www.unhcr.org/4ab356ab6.pdf

Vapattanawong, Patama. (2017). *Foreigners in Thailand*. Institute for Population and Social Research – Mahidol University, Bangkok.

Willen, Sarah S. 2007. 'Toward a Critical Phenomenology of 'Illegality': State Power, Criminalization, and Abjectivity among Undocumented Migrant Workers in Tel Aviv, Israel,' *International Migration*, 45 (3), pp. 8–38.

Winichakul, Thongchai. (2000). 'The Others Within,' in Turton, Andrew (ed), *Civility and Savagery*, pp. 38–62. London: Curzon Press.

World Refugee Council. (2019). *A Call to Action. Transforming the Global Refugee System*. Available at: https://www.cigionline.org/sites/default/files/documents/ WRC_Call_to_Action.pdf

# 5 Escaping Al-Shabaab and seeking safety in Thailand

## Somalis in Bangkok

*George Kiarie*

### Introduction

Over the last 30 years, hundreds of thousands of people have fled Somalia because of political instability and a dangerous civil war that broke out in the 1990s. According to the UN High Commissioner for Refugees (UNHCR), some 750,000 Somali refugees remain in neighboring countries and over 2.6 million Somalis are internally displaced in Somalia (see Avis & Herbert 2016).

Initially, the refugees fled to the neighboring countries of Kenya (256,186), Ethiopia (192,082), and Yemen (250,500), where many still remain. The largest concentration of Somalis is in the Horn of Africa and Yemen, Gulf States, Western Europe, and North America. In Europe, the United Kingdom is home to the largest Somali community, followed by the Netherlands, Norway, Sweden, and Denmark. Somali asylum seekers have also settled in Switzerland. Malaysia and Australia have also seen a number of Somali immigrants in recent years. In the United States, Minnesota is home to the largest Somali community, with the majority residing in the Minneapolis–St. Paul metropolitan area, as well as St. Cloud and Rochester. Many Somali refugees and immigrants have also settled in the Seattle metropolitan area and Columbus, Ohio.

The displacement of Somalis continues. Flash flooding and riverine flooding in the southern regions of Somalia have displaced over 650,000 Somalis in the first eight months of 2020. Many of the newly displaced are now living in overcrowded, makeshift shelters in already dire sites for the internally displaced (IDPs). Sanitary conditions in the shelters are poor and access to medical care is scarce; the shelters provide little to no protection from the harsh weather and they leave families exposed to increased risk of crimes. Ongoing droughts in central and northern Somalia and flooding during the rainy season in southern and central Somalia have left 4.8 million people food insecure. Around 2.1 million

DOI: 10.4324/9781003286554-5

people face acute food insecurity, while 1.1 million children under age five are acutely malnourished (Bentley 2020).

COVID-19 has disproportionately affected the Somali population. In June 2020, Somali authorities confirmed over 2,100 cases of COVID-19, but it is believed there are thousands of undetected infections due to limited testing capacity. Humanitarians are concerned about the impact of the pandemic on the country's highly vulnerable population, including the internally displaced. According to RAND, Somalia is the most vulnerable country in the world for infectious diseases. The country is already in the midst of a cholera outbreak. While the worldwide standard is around 25 healthcare workers per 100,000 people, Somalia has only two. There is only one hospital in the entire country capable of treating coronavirus patients. Al-Shabab has exploited the virus for political gains by claiming that it was spread 'by the crusader forces who have invaded the country and the disbelieving countries that support them' (Bentley 2020). Given the unstable political situation in the failed state and natural and man-made disasters, many Somalis continue to seek safety and livelihood opportunities outside the country (USA for UNHCR 2020).

Finding Somalis in Thailand is something of a surprise. Bangkok is a cosmopolitan city, but has very few Black residents. Precise statistical data on Africans living in Thailand is scarce. According to the UN High Commissioner for Refugees (UNHCR), 8,166 Africans were living in the country in 2010. In 2017, 223 Somalis applied for asylum in Thailand, while in 2018, 230 Somalis launched asylum applications in Bangkok. The approval rates decreased drastically from 60 percent in 2017 to 17 percent in 2018 (UNHCR 2018).

In this chapter, I use case studies of three Somalis who left Beledweyne in south-central Somalia where the Al-Shabaab, a jihadist fundamentalist group, attacks and terrorizes the local population, to illustrate three different ways of seeking safety and better prospects in Bangkok. The protagonists of this chapter include an asylum seeker, a graduate student, and a businessman.

Thailand is not a signatory of the 1951 Refugee Convention nor does it have any special immigration provisions for African asylum seekers or immigrants. The Somali migrants have to find creative ways of making a living and surviving in Bangkok. I explore their coping strategies and engage with the issue of being Black in a country that has few Black people, and being Muslim in a predominantly Buddhist country. This chapter provides a platform for the studied individuals to voice their aspirations and future plans. Hopefully, these voices will be taken into account as Thai policy-makers consider ways to admit migrants on humanitarian grounds.

I begin by introducing the three protagonists whose narratives inform my chapter. A discussion of immigration policies (or lack of such) that frame the integration processes of Somalis residing in Bangkok follows. The bulk of the chapter is devoted to the presentation of empirical findings. First, I focus on the flight from Somalia and the arrival in Thailand. I also discuss the legal and economic precarity the protagonists face. I situate the discussion of precarity at the nexus of being Muslim and Black as these two factors contribute to the challenges faced by the protagonists of this chapter.

## The protagonists

I purposefully selected Khadija, an asylum seeker, Farooq, an international student, and Abdi, a businessman, as their experiences are representative of three different migration and integration trajectories. While they each chose different paths to come to Thailand, they shared common experiences in Somalia. All three fled Beledweyne in south-central Somalia where Al-Shabaab, a jihadist fundamentalist group, attacks and terrorizes the local population. All three expressed fear of being persecuted by the terrorist group.

Khadija is a young female and an asylum seeker in Thailand. At the time of our interview, she was 19 and lived in Thailand for three years. Khadija has no formal education and is an orphan. In Somalia, she stayed with her aunt. They survived on remittances sent by the aunt's adult children residing in the United States. Khadija belongs to the Asharaf religious minority. The followers believe themselves to be descendants of the daughter of the prophet Muhammed. Khadija said: 'I believe that we are descendants of Fatimah bint Muhammad who was the youngest daughter of the Prophet Mohammed.' According to Khadija, members of her clan were discriminated against by the larger communities that have formed Al-Shabaab. According to the US Department of Justice, this group is indeed subjected to abuse at the hands of non-state actors and society at large. Members of minority groups who live in the southern and central parts of Somalia, a particularly unstable part of the country, appear to bear the brunt of the abuse (Goitom 2016).

Farooq is a 31-year-old male. He is pursuing a master's degree in peace studies and diplomacy at Siam University on a partial scholarship. He too comes from Beledweyne. Farooq described the suffering resulting from a devastating war and clashes between the Ethiopia-backed Somali Transition Federal Government and Al-Shabaab. Farooq narrated these events as leading to general insecurity and fear of persecution among Somalis living in the area. Additionally, Al-Shabaab required young Somalis to collaborate with the group. Farooq was afraid that he would not survive recruitment and would end up being executed by the militia.

Abdi is a 42-year-old man with a bachelor's degree in commerce. He said: 'At home, my parents instilled values of entrepreneurship in me and that encouraged me to study commerce at Hope University in Mogadishu. I wanted to be able to help my siblings.' Abdi runs a small foreign currency exchange and remittance-sending bureau. He caters mainly to other Africans. He said: 'Most of my clients are Africans. Be it tourists or businessmen, they prefer my shop to others. Perhaps it's Black unity.' He also sends clothes to his family in Somalia and Kenya to sell for profit. Abdi fled Somalia because of terrorist attacks led by Al-Shabaab, fueled by clannism. Abdi cites the Issa clan as the main problem in his home area because of their desire for power and lack of willingness to collaborate with other clans.

## Policy frameworks and cultural context

Despite the presence of refugees and asylum seekers, Thailand is neither signatory to the 1951 UN Convention relating to the Status of Refugees nor its 1967 Protocol and 'lacks legal and administrative frameworks for identifying and protecting refugees' (Palmgren 2013: 24). There is also no formal national asylum framework for distinguishing refugees and asylum seekers from other undocumented migrants (Lego 2018). Thailand is not alone in this regard. This lack of appropriate protection mechanisms for refugees and asylum seekers is reflective of the broader refugee protection landscape within the Association of Southeast Asian Nations (ASEAN), where only two countries – Cambodia and the Philippines – are signatories to the relevant UN conventions.

The majority of refugees in Thailand live in refugee camps near the Thai–Myanmar border. In 2006, the Border Consortium (TBC) recorded more than 153,000 refugees and asylum seekers living in nine border camps (The Border Consortium 2007 cited in Lego 2018). Under the Thai Immigration Act of 1979, refugees and asylum seekers not admitted to the camps are lumped in with all undocumented migrants. They are considered 'illegal economic migrants' and are subject to arrest, detention, and deportation. In 2012, the Jesuit Refugee Services (JRS) estimated that some 2,000 urban refugees were living in Bangkok (Jesuit Refugee Services 2012). In 2016, Asylum Access, a legal aid organization in Bangkok, put the number of urban refugees in the city at 8,000+ (Asylum Access 2016). This trend shows that more and more refugees seek safety in Thailand. Without legal protection, these refugees and asylum seekers live precarious lives as noticed by many refugee advocacy organizations (Human Rights Watch 2012; Jesuit Refugee Services 2012; USCRI 2006).

In 2017, the Thai government started to formalize the screening procedure for asylum seekers (UNHCR 2018). However, despite the establishment of formal screening, the refugee status determination (RSD) process for African refugees is lengthy and only provides limited protection. In theory, urban refugees who have registered with UNHCR are recognized by the Thai Government as 'persons of concern to UNHCR.' As such, they are eligible for resettlement in third countries and will not be expelled from Thailand (Huguet & Punpuing 2005; see also Chantavanich & Jitpong, this issue). However, because of racial prejudices, many African asylum seekers are discriminated against by authorities and end up in detention (see Unor & Thabchumpon, this volume). Authorities arrested more than 1,000 suspected visa violators under operation *X-Ray Outlaw Foreigners*, launched in 2017. 'The suspicious targets are the dark-skinned people. First, we search their bodies, then we search their passports,' an official stated before sending out about 75 officers on an evening round-up of more suspects. 'Thailand's immigration crackdown has swept up refugees and asylum seekers, sent young children into horrid, prison-like conditions, and appears to have clear aspects of racial profiling against South Asians and Africans,' said Brad Adams, Asia director at the Human Rights Watch (NewsOne 2018). The fate of African migrants very much depends on the mercy of the Thai government (Frelick & Saltsman 2012).

The three protagonists of this chapter are part of the urban refugee population in Thailand and have to face these harsh challenges. Additionally, they are Black and Muslim. According to the 2015 Thai Census, 4.2 percent of Thailand's population is Muslim. Thailand's Muslim population is diverse, with ethnic groups having migrated from China, Pakistan, India, Cambodia, Bangladesh, Malaysia, and Indonesia. There are also Muslim ethnic Thais, but the majority of Muslims in Thailand are Thai Malays. There were no Black Muslims in the country up until 1970 when Africans started arriving in Thailand.

Most Thai people have never encountered people of African descent. Prejudice and stereotypes about people of African descent were absorbed by Thais through the Vietnam War and Western literature and movies (Draper et al. 2019). Racism and prejudice against Blacks are reported in the media (Eromosele 2015). As late as 2016, the common brands featuring people of African descent included mops, toilet brushes, and toothpaste (Under the Ropes 2016). There is also a fairly devastating first-person account of racial prejudices against a Black anthropologist working within the UN system (Tegbaru 2020). Lack of legal protections coupled with racism, prejudice, and discrimination pose serious challenges for Somalis as they try to survive in Thai society.

## Flight and arrival in Thailand

Somali migrants started arriving in Thailand in the late 1980s. They originally came in search of safe haven from the armed conflict, but they used different strategies to reach the country. They settled mainly in the Bangkok suburbs.

Khadija fled Somalia because her life was in danger. She refused to join Al-Shabaab. She said: 'Al-Shabaab needs women to cook for them and use them as spies. Once you refuse to abide by their will, they consider you a traitor and they will kill you.' Khadija described how the insurgent group wanted to control her town of Kismayo that had also been controlled by Kenyan and African Union Mission in Somalia (AMISOM) troops. Al-Shabaab was lacking soldiers, therefore, they requested every young person, man or woman, in the area to join them 'for their victory.' She narrated her experience with one of the Al-Shabaab leaders as follows:

> One of the Al-Shabaab leaders tried to hand me a gun. He said that if he were me, young and healthy, he would be at the front line of the battle and not at home. Al-Shabab targets predominantly marginalized youth and orphans, however, even those who do not fit into those categories are not immune from recruitment. The fact that I was a girl and an orphan encouraged them to coerce me. They even threatened that if I failed to join them; they would kill me just like they kill all the rebels.

As Al-Shabaab was encroaching on her hometown, Khadija decided to flee Somalia fearing her life was in danger. A smuggler facilitated her journey to Thailand. Khadija was introduced to the smuggler through one of her aunts. Khadija flew from Somalia through Dubai to Malaysia. The smuggler advised her not to leave the plane until it landed in Kuala Lumpur. After landing in KL, Khadija contacted another smuggler who was waiting for her at the airport. Once she got her tourist visa, the agent helped her book a bus to Thailand. Upon reaching Bangkok, Khadija contacted yet another man who directed her to a cheap room in Bang Na.

Khadija was 16 years old when she arrived in Bangkok in 2014. The journey was costly. Khadija's aunt mobilized all her relatives abroad to pay for the trip. The cost of the trip was closely tied to the use of fraudulent travel documents. Khadija reported paying the smugglers a total of US$7,000. Following the advice of her cousins living abroad, she paid everybody in cash: $6,000 to the agency that arranged the trip and an additional $1,000 to cover the cost of rent, food, and clothing.

It is not entirely clear from Khadija's description who the recipients of the money were and whether the money covered legitimate fees (airfare) or whether these were bribes. For the Somalis trying to escape Somalia, smuggling networks, social networks, and financial resources are the main elements needed to travel to Thailand. Smuggling networks charge anywhere between $3,000 and $5,000 per person to facilitate a clandestine migration out of Somalia (Koser 2008). Malaysia and Indonesia were important transit points for the Indo-Chinese boat people in the 1980s and 1990s, but today Malaysia is still used by many Muslim migrants from Africa and the Middle East. Malaysia, in particular, has become an 'entry point' for asylum seekers, as it offers tourist visas on arrival to passengers from more than 60 countries in order to boost its tourism (Missbach & Sinanu 2011). Upon arrival in Malaysia, Somali migrants contact relatives or friends for further information necessary to continue travel to the destination country (United Nations 2000).

Abdi's migration trajectory was quite different. He left Somalia for the same reasons Khadija left. Abdi is also a member of a minority group, the Bravanese clan. Abdi said that the situation for minority groups worsened when the armed conflict became full-blown in both Somaliland and south Somalia. The Bravanese suffered severe human rights violations, including extrajudicial killings, appropriation of land and properties, and forced displacement to refugee camps situated along the Somali–Ethiopian border. He narrated the fate of his clan:

> Most of my clan members, including my relatives, had been killed by Al-Shabaab who considered us sympathizers and collaborators with their enemy. I lived in fear and I had to run to save my life. Killing to them was the order of the day.

Abdi and his family relocated first to Kenya, where he was then able to buy a Kenyan identity card. Having two passports served him well when he decided to go to Thailand and start a business. 'You know,' he said, 'corruption sometimes is good and sometimes bad. I was referred to a person in Kenya whom I paid a huge amount of money in order to get citizenship for myself and my wife.' Having a Kenyan passport, albeit fraudulent, enabled Abdi to enjoy the freedoms and rights of a Kenyan citizen. This included the right to travel as a 'Kenyan.' He simply hopped on a plane and flew from Nairobi to Bangkok where he received a 90-day tourist visa on arrival.

Farooq arrived in Thailand in 2013 as an international student. A family friend who lives in Bangkok helped deliver his application to the university where Farooq wanted to study. The war and political instability were the reasons Farooq wanted to leave Somalia. Farooq described the devastation of his village caused by the prolonged armed conflict. Most of the residents in his village were farmers, but farming is no longer feasible as the land is devastated or farms are appropriated by Al-Shabaab. Farooq did not see any prospects for himself if he stayed in Somalia. Having enough educational capital to enroll in a university, he chose to pursue higher education as the escape route. He selected Thailand specifically because the university offers a scholarship that covers 50 percent of his tuition and school fees. Additionally, Farooq's brother works for an international organization and supports him in Thailand.

Getting to Thailand is but one step in the long journey refugees face. Staying in Bangkok and securing a decent livelihood is a different story. In the next section, I will look at the elements that contribute to the precarious situations all three protagonists face.

## Living a precarious life

In migration studies, precarity is usually theorized in relation to the most vulnerable migrants. It is often associated with low wages, 'illegality,' and 'deportability' (Menjívar & Kanstroom 2013; Paret & Gleeson 2016). Migration scholars use precarity to describe particular groups of migrants frequently working without work permits and as a result facing various abuses (Isaksen 2010) or forced migrants who live in 'liminal zones, waiting for borders to open, food to arrive, and the prospect of living with documentation' (Butler 2016: 201). Marcel Paret and Shannon Gleeson emphasize that migrant existence is often precarious in multiple and reinforcing ways, combining vulnerability to deportation and state violence, exclusion from public services and basic state protections, insecure employment and exploitation at work, insecure livelihood, and everyday discrimination or isolation (Paret & Gleeson 2016). Asylum seekers in Thailand who overstay their tourist visas or who have entered the country without documentation are not allowed to work or gain access to education and as a result, are forced to live largely invisible lives on the margins of Thai society. They live in constant fear of arrest, detention, and deportation. Lack of work permits also affects their economic self-sufficiency.

### *Legal precarity*

Khadija's situation in Bangkok is certainly precarious. She registered with UNHCR and applied for a refugee status hoping that she will have a chance to be resettled in the West, perhaps in Minnesota where some of her family members live. Unfortunately, UNHCR did not find her application to be credible and her claim was rejected. Khadija appealed the decision and at the time of our interview was awaiting the results of her appeal. She received an identity card labeled 'A' (asylum seeker) from UNHCR. In contrast to those who have UNHCR cards with the letter 'R' (refugee), Khadija's identity card does not accord her much protection in Thailand. She said: 'If I had the other identity card labeled 'R' this would mean that I am a refugee. Holding a refugee card is much more secure than having the asylum seeker's card for it minimizes chances of arrest.' Having an 'R' card Khadija would be able to access education, medical care, and social protection services. Lack of proper documentation does not allow Khadija to move freely around the city, even when she needs to seek assistance. 'Life in Bangkok hasn't been so easy,' she said. 'Leaving my room increases my chances of detention. It means that when I am sick, I cannot visit the hospital for I do not have documents proving my legality.' Legal precarity accords Khadija few rights and limits her access to services, including healthcare.

Abdi came to Thailand six years ago on a tourist visa to start a small business. For the first three years, he continued to leave Thailand for Malaysia every three months in order to obtain a re-entry visa. Currently, he has a business permit that allows him to stay in Thailand legally without needing to constantly renew his visa. Abdi described the journey to Malaysia as expensive and at the same time tedious. It is not guaranteed to get a visa back to Thailand, so he had to find a way to make his stay 'legal.' A business partnership that he established with a Thai friend spared him the expensive travels to Malaysia. With a Thai business partner, Abdi is authorized to live and conduct business in Thailand. Abdi has hopes of expanding his business to Canada or China. It seems that Abdi's situation is less precarious than Khadija's, at least as long as he has a Thai business partner. Abdi did not share much information about how he splits his profits with the Thai partner, but I assume it must be financially advantageous to both of them.

Farooq has a student visa that enables him to study and live in Thailand legally. Obtaining a student visa, however, was not done without several difficulties. There is no Thai embassy in Somalia, therefore, Farooq had to go to Nairobi to pick up his visa. It took almost eight weeks for the Thai embassy to confirm that his visa was ready. Farooq was lucky to have family members living in Kenya who were able to host him as he made his visa arrangements. Farooq has to renew his student visa once in a while and the process is problematic as it requires money and time. He has to report to the immigration office in person and often wait the whole day to see an immigration officer. Farooq intends to settle in Thailand or to emigrate to the United States. He explained that he plans on enrolling in another bachelor's degree that would last more than three years to graduate. This would help him buy more time to legally stay in Thailand and maybe find a better way of relocating to North America. These plans seem quite unrealistic. Farooq is already in his 30s; will he find another scholarship to pay for his continued studies? Unfortunately, his dream of going to the United States is still just a dream. Refugee admissions resumed once the Biden administration was installed, but Farooq would need to first register with UNHCR and be deemed a *bona fide* refugee before he could apply for resettlement in the United States.

While Khadija's immigration situation is the most precarious, both Abdi and Farooq face challenges as well, especially if they want to continue doing business and living in Thailand. It's worthwhile mentioning that Thailand has started to develop mechanisms to support and protect refugees following the promise the Prime Minister made at the UN General Assembly in 2016, but nothing is in place yet.

### Economic precarity

In addition to legal precarity, all three protagonists experience economic precarity. Khadija's economic situation is as precarious as her immigration status. She receives a monthly stipend of 2,000 THB from UNHCR. She scrapes rent money from remittances sent by her relatives. She also serves as an interpreter with a local NGO, but since she doesn't have a work permit, this is not a proper waged job. Even with a work permit, Khadija would not be easily employable. She has no formal education and speaks very little Thai. 'Poverty was the greatest hindrance to my education,' she told me. 'My aunt had no money. To make matters worse, bias towards boys makes women's education, not a priority. In fact, educating a woman is seen as a waste of resources.' Khadija contextualized her own poverty within the broader Somali society as follows:

> In Kismaiyo, all economic sources such as the seaport, airport, and commercial activities are all controlled by the Habregedir and Marehan clans. Those who do not belong to these groups, and particularly the Asheraf clan to which I belong, can work only as underpaid servants. In Kismaiyo, the dominant clans control the economy. Minorities occupy subordinate roles.

The Thai government does not provide any financial support for asylum seekers despite proclaiming political support for asylum seekers (Park 2020). The international community does not seem to have any plans to support asylum seekers in Thailand either. Is this compassion fatigue? 'Where does that leave me as an asylum seeker?' asked Khadija. Indeed, it seems highly likely Khadija could become food insecure and possibly homeless should her family not be able to continue to send money.

Abdi is doing fine economically, at least for the moment. At first, he focused more on buying clothes in Thailand and selling them in Somalia and Kenya. However, the clothes business is quite competitive as many

Africans are also engaged in exporting cheap clothing. The money-sending business, however, is less competitive. According to Abdi, not many Africans have the capital to invest in such a business. Abdi is thinking about expanding his business and having one of his relatives manage the current money-sending bureau, while he takes on another. He is proud of his achievements:

> Today I have achieved something in my life. I have my own business and succeeded to do something good for my family. My business is accepted. I started my business from zero and now I'm in a very good position here in Thailand.

Although optimistic, Abdi might be overestimating his success as his business depends highly on having a Thai partner. Also, he does not have enough resources to both send money to his family and visit them. Instead, he uses all of his money to provide for his wife and six children.

Farooq has no formal job. However, he can get part-time interpretation and translation jobs in Arabic and Somali through friends. These jobs do not pay much because he has no work permit. Lack of a work permit limits his ability to make money and puts him at risk of being found by local authorities. I have also wondered whether he realizes that working under the table might jeopardize his student visa and his scholarship. Farooq relies on the money his brother sends. None of the strategies the protagonists deploy are sustainable in the long run. There is always the danger that relatives will no longer be able to send remittances.

## Survival strategies

Given the precarious situation they find themselves in, Khadija, Abdi, and Farooq deploy different strategies to survive in Bangkok. While all three are very visible because of the color of their skin, Khadija felt that wearing a hijab made her more at risk for being detained. In order to partially obscure her Black Muslim identity, Khadija decided to start wearing Western clothes. 'I am a Muslim woman,' she told me,

> But here in Bangkok streets, you can't tell if I'm one. I wear clothes just like any other modern woman. In Somalia, I would be wearing a long hijab but not because I wanted to but rather because it is what society expected of me.

The Western clothes helped Khadija feel emancipated and enabled her to mingle with people of different cultures. Khadija feels more secure in her Western clothes. She said: 'Most of our clothing covers the entire face and, in a way, it is not well accepted by non-Muslim people, who think that Muslims pose a security threat.' Despite abandoning the outward religious symbols, Khadija gains strength from her religion. Khadija said that what gives meaning to her life is religion: 'Religion is important to every Muslim because we learn to share and help each other.' Khadija attends Friday Jummah prayers at the local mosque to observe religious practices as well as to socialize with other Muslim women.

In order to survive, Khadija is also learning Thai. She teaches herself using her phone. She is determined to learn English as she feels knowing English would make her more employable. Although accustomed to poverty in Somalia, Khadija said her economic situation in Bangkok is dire. Despite the odds, she tries to make ends meet.

Abdi relies on the African network in Bangkok both for his business and moral and social support. He recalled the time when he first arrived in Bangkok: 'Six years ago when I arrived in Bangkok, I asked almost every African I found about the presence of Somalis until I found one.' He indicated he wasn't alone in wanting to connect with fellow Somalis; all newly arrived Somalis look for their countrymen. When I asked him why, he said that it creates a sense of belonging. Whenever he meets other Somalis, he feels at home because they have so much in common, including the language. Abdi's business benefits from the African networks because African immigrants are his main clientele. In order to integrate professionally and socially, Abdi learned Thai. He thinks it is a good investment in his future as he plans to stay in Thailand for a while and expand his business. Abdi said Somali people are nomads and they will always be on the move, so he expects more Somalis to come to Thailand. I wonder how this will be possible without any legal ways of obtaining a residence permit.

Farooq tries to integrate into the Thai society through football. He loves the sport and has joined a local football team. Farooq thinks about football as a way to secure his future in Thailand. He hopes that if he is picked up by a local football club, he will be able to invest in a small business exporting cosmetics to Somalia. He expects that profits from a small cosmetics enterprise would sustain him in Thailand and also support his extended family back home. His long-term plan is to get permanent residency provided he succeeds as a professional footballer. This possibility would help him to bring his family members. An alternative plan is to become a professional interpreter and be hired by UNHCR or a local NGO. He is also considering opening an interpretation service. These are all very ambitious plans, but perhaps not as realistic as Farooq thinks.

## Conclusions

Unless the Thai government passes humanitarian laws allowing asylum seekers to gain some rights – either on a temporary or permanent basis – Khadija, Farooq, and Abdi face rather bleak integration prospects.

Khadija's legal situation is the most critical. Having failed to obtain a refugee status, she has no hope for resettlement in a third country and no legal status in Thailand. Once he has completed his studies, Farooq might have good employment prospects, but his limited knowledge of Thai does not bode well for finding a job in Thailand, unless he works for an international company. Being a person of color, his chances are further diminished. I have not seen any Black people working outside the ethnic community. Most Africans I encountered either work for themselves or for other Africans, in restaurants, small African-owned stores, and beauty salons. Abdi's entrepreneurial spirit is probably the best hope he has, although his continued presence in Thailand hinges on sustaining his partnership with the Thai businessman.

It seems that Thai authorities should be interested in providing African migrants with a legal solution that would enable them to continue to be productive members of the Thai society. All three of the protagonists are either already economically productive (Abdi) or have the potential to be contributing members of the host society (Farooq with his educational capital and Khadija with her determination to fit in and learn Thai). While humanitarian law would benefit asylum seekers from Africa, expansion of labor laws to allow Africans to work in Thailand would also benefit Africans and Thai society. Thailand's vibrant economy and rising living standards attract legions of migrant workers. The migrants are a valuable source of labor for Thailand, which began industrializing rapidly in the 1980s, helped by foreign investment and a resource boom. The country's economic development pulled Thai workers out of farming, fishing, and construction and into manufacturing. More than 3.3 million foreign nationals work in Thailand and make up 10 percent of its workforce. As the country ages, it is growing increasingly dependent on foreign labor (Ono 2019; see also Tipayalai 2020). However, the vast majority of the migrant workers are from neighboring countries.

At the moment, African migrants rely mainly on their own resiliency, or in the case of the Muslim Somalis, also on their local mosques. The Imam

I interviewed indicated that there the number of Somali asylum seekers has grown in the past five years. The mosque decided to set up a foundation that helps vulnerable Somali Muslims. Muslim doctors and nurses provide medical assistance and the foundation also collects donations to offer food and provide 1,000 THB to offset the cost of rent. The mosque also provides spiritual and social support. However, a reliance on charity limits the migrants' ability to lead decent lives.

## References

Asylum Access. (2016). *Urban Refugees in Bangkok.* Available at: https://asylumaccess.org/urban-refugees-bangkok/

Avis, William & Siân, Herbert. (2016). *Rapid Fragility and Migration Assessment for Somalia.* Birmingham: GSDRC, University of Birmingham.

Bentley, Arden. (2020). 'The Humanitarian Disaster Before Us: COVID-19 in Somalia,' *Refugees International*, 8 June. Available at: https://www.refugeesinternational.org/reports/2020/6/8/the-humanitarian-disaster-before-us-covid-19-in-somalia

Butler, Judith. (2016). *Towards a Performative Theory of Assembly.* Cambridge, MA: Harvard University Press.

Draper, John, Sobieszczyk, Teresa, Crumpton, Charles D., Lefferts, H. L., & Chachavalpongpun, Pavin. (2019). 'Racial "Othering" in Thailand: Quantitative Evidence, Causes, and Consequences,' *Nationalism and Ethnic Politics*, 25 (3), pp. 251–72. doi: 10.1080/13537113.2019.1639425

Eromosele, Diana Ozemebhoya. (2015). 'Being Black in Thailand: We're Treated Better Than Africans and Boy Do We Hate It,' *The Root*, 12 January. Available at: https://www.theroot.com/being-black-in-thailand-we-re-treated-better-than-afri-1790859954

Frelick, Bill & Adam Saltsman. 2012. *Ad hoc and Inadequate: Thailand's Treatment of Refugees and Asylum Seekers.* New York: Human Rights Watch.

Goitom, Hanibal. (2016). *Somalia: Treatment of Religious Minorities.* Report for the U.S. Department of Justice LL File No. 2016-013913. Available at: https://www.justice.gov/eoir/file/884961/download

Huguet, Jerrold W. & Punpuing, Sureeporn. (2005). *International Migration in Thailand.* Bangkok: International Organization for Migration (IOM).

Human Rights Watch. (2012). *Ad Hoc and Inadequate: Thailand's Treatment of Refugees and Asylum Seekers.* Available at: https://www.hrw.org/sites/default/files/reports/thailand0912.pdf

Isaksen, Lise W. (2010). *Global Care Work: Gender and Migration in Nordic Societies.* Lund: Nordic Academic Press.

Jesuit Refugee Services. (2012). *The Search: Protection Space in Malaysia, Thailand, Indonesia, Cambodia and the Philippines.* Thailand: JRS Asia Pacific.

72 *George Kiarie*

Koser, Khalid. (2008). 'Why Migrant Smuggling Pays,' *International Migration*, 46 (2), pp. 3–26. doi: 10.1111/j.1468-2435.2008.00442.x

Lego, Jera. (2018). 'Making Refugees (Dis)appear: Identifying Refugees and Asylum Seekers in Thailand and Malaysia,' *Austrian Journal of South-East Asian Studies*, 11 (2), pp. 183–98.

Menjívar, Cecilia & Kanstroom, Dan. (2013). *Constructing Immigrant 'Illegality'. Critiques, Experiences, and Responses*. Cambridge: Cambridge University Press.

Missbach, Antje & Sinanu, Frieda. (2011). 'The Scum of the Earth? Foreign People Smugglers and Their Local Counterparts in Indonesia,' *Journal of Current Southeast Asian Affairs*, 30 (4), pp. 57–87.

NewsOne. (2018). 'Thailand Tells Black People Don't Come Here,' *NewsOne*, 22 October. Available at: https://newsone.com/3832864/thailand-immigration-crackdown-dark-skinned-people/

Ono, Yukako. (2019). 'Migrant Workers in Thailand Live Harsh, but Improving, Reality Bangkok Takes Legal Steps to Retain Vital Laborers from Neighboring Countries,' *Nikkei Asia*, 17 February. Available at: https://asia.nikkei.com/Life-Arts/Life/Migrant-workers-in-Thailand-live-harsh-but-improving-reality

Palmgren, Pei A. (2013). 'Irregular Networks: Bangkok Refugees in the City and Region,' *Journal of Refugee Studies*, 27 (1), pp. 21–41.

Paret, Marcel & Gleeson, Shannon. (2016). 'Precarity and Agency through a Migration Lens,' *Citizenship Studies*, 20 (3–4), pp. 277–94.

Park, Min Jee Yamada. (2020). 'Thailand's National Screening Mechanism Paves the Way for Better Refugee Protection,' *International Detention Coalition*, 7 February. Available at: https://reliefweb.int/report/thailand/thailand-s-national-screening-mechanism-paves-way-better-refugee-protection

Tegbaru, Amare. (2020). 'The Racialization of Development Expertise and the Fluidity of Blackness: A Case from 1980s Thailand,' *Asian Anthropology*, 19 (3), pp. 195–212. doi: 10.1080/1683478X.2020.1713288

Tipayalai, Katikar. (2020). 'Impact of International Labor Migration on Regional Economic Growth in Thailand,' *Economic Structures*, 9 (15), pp. 1–19. doi: 10.1186/s40008-020-00192-7

Under the Ropes. (2016). 'Blackface and Racism in Thailand,' *Under the Ropes*, 22 January. Available at: https://undertheropes.com/2016/01/22/blackface-and-racism-in-thailand/

UNHCR. (2018). *Population Statistics Database*. Available at: https://www.unhcr.org/refugee-statistics/

United Nations. (2000). *Protocol against the Smuggling of Migrants by Land, Sea and Air, Supplementing the United Nations Convention against Transnational Organized Crime*. Available at: https://www.unodc.org/documents/middleeastandnorthafrica/smuggling-migrants/SoM_Protocol_English.pdf

USA for UNHCR. (2020). *Somalia Refugee Crisis Explained.* Available at: https://www.unrefugees.org/news/somalia-refugee-crisis-explained/#:~:text =Over%20the%20last%2030%20years,are%20internally%20displaced%20in %20Somalia

USCRI. 2006. *U.S. Committee for Refugees and Immigrants World Refugee Survey 2006–Malaysia.* Available at: https://www.refworld.org/docid/4496ad0a3e.html

# 6 Being Black and trying to survive in a niche economy

## Nigerian traders in Bangkok

*Anthony Unor and Naruemon Thabchumpon*

## Introduction

Migration from Nigeria to Thailand started in the 1980s (Patin 2012). Many Nigerians left their homeland because of political instability and human rights abuses perpetrated by military regimes; others went in search of better livelihoods. Most Nigerians who first immigrated to Thailand took advantage of the booming rice trade (Titapiwatanakun & Titapiwatanakun 2012) and the import and export of clothes and gemstones. Nigerians who arrived later came to play professional football, teach English, pursue higher education on scholarships provided by the Thai government (Patin 2012), and seek romance (marriage).

Initially, Nigerians followed a circular migration trajectory and preferred short sojourns to long-term settlement (Kalu 2007). However, with time, some desired to settle. Although Thailand is home to 4.9 million migrants, it is not an immigration country. Most of the migrants in Thailand are contract workers from neighboring countries. The assumption is that they will return home once their contracts end (OECD/ILO 2017). At the moment, there are no provisions for asylum seekers from the Association of Southeast Asian Nations (ASEAN) (see Chantavanich, this volume). As a result, African migrants who want to settle in Thailand are left with very few options.

Bangkok, followed by Pattaya, Phuket, and Hat Yai, are the favorite destinations for Nigerian migrants. Currently, the Nigerian diaspora in Thailand is estimated at 1,400 persons. The majority are men between 25 and 55 years of age. Women constitute ten percent of the population (Judd 2018).

Nigerians have made many contributions to Thai society and have been rewarded for their achievements: Dr. Uche Veronica Amazigo, former director of WHO's African Program for Onchocerciasis Control (APOC), won the 2012 Prince Mahidol Award in public health (Fernquest 2012a); Ettah Emmanuel won an award at the 2020 Bangkok International Education Summit; Auwal Bala Abubakar of Chulalongkorn University

DOI: 10.4324/9781003286554-6

won Thailand's Highest Journal Citation in 2021 (Clifford 2020; Ewubare 2021).

Despite these achievements, Nigerians residing in Thailand face persistent discrimination and racism (Colbey 2018; Ehrlich 2020). Lack of understanding of the diversity of African people frequently leads to stereotyping African migrants (Nwabueze 2017; Rojanaphruk 2020). A significant percentage of Thais do not want to live next to a Black person (Gye 2013). According to an International Labor Organization (ILO) survey, 78 percent of Thai people attribute a high number of crimes to migrants, especially Africans. Approximately 58 percent believe migrants are a threat to Thai cultural heritage. Colbey (2018) and Thaitrakulpanich (2020) show that racially motivated arrests make daily life a constant struggle for Africans in Thailand. Thai law enforcement perceives Africans as criminals despite international research suggesting otherwise (Özden, Testaverde, and Wagner 2015, cited in World Bank 2015).

Discrimination against Nigerians peaked in 2018 when ten Africans were arrested during *Operation Black Eagle*. The Thai Tourist Police Chief said at the time: '[r]oughly 1,400 Nigerians … were investigated and questioned about their income to prevent further crimes committed by foreigners.' However, the police spokesperson rebuffed allegations of racial discrimination stating that race-based discrimination goes against the tenet of policing globally (Judd 2018).

Negative perceptions of Nigerians stem not only from media narratives but also intersect with Thai superstitions that equate black with sadness (Sakaowan & Ruiz, 2014), lower status, poverty, and ugliness (BBC 2016). These superstitions – combined with anti-migrant sentiments, views about the history of Africa (colonialism and slavery), and assessments of African development (weak and fragile states, sickness, and poverty) – result in various forms of racism against Nigerians in Thailand (Eromosele 2015).

Using empirical research with Nigerian traders in Bangkok, we analyze how encounters with Nigerian migrants contribute to the ways representatives of the Thai government, media, and the wider society construe cultural representations of the African 'Other.' We explore how these representations affect Thais' attitudes towards Black Africans living in Thailand and identify the challenges Nigerian entrepreneurs face as they try to integrate into the Thai business community and wider society. We situate our discussion within the theoretical framework of 'othering' and analyze our findings at the intersection of race, illegality, and gender (in this case, masculinity).

Many scholars have theorized 'otherness' and the process of 'othering' (e.g., Beauvoir 1952; Fanon 1963; Duncan 1993; Said 2016; Sibley 2007). They agree that to be othered is to be denied the fullness of one's humanity (Grant-Thomas 2016; Kerrison et al. 2018; Staszak 2008, Udah 2019).

According to Michel Foucault, othering is strongly connected with power and knowledge. When we 'other' another group, we point out their perceived weaknesses to make ourselves look stronger or better. It implies a hierarchy, and it serves to keep power where it already lies. Colonialism is one such example of the powers of othering (Foucault 1970). Our analysis rests on the premise that Thai models of 'The Other' constitute what Clyde Kluckhohn once described as 'cultural portraits of ourselves' (Kluckhohn 1962); thereby, our research provides nuanced portraits of both Thais and the African immigrants they encounter.

Intersectionality, a term coined by Kimberlé Crenshaw (1991), describes a lens that allows us to see where power comes and collides, where it interlocks and intersects. It's not simply that there's a race problem here, a gender problem here, and a class or LBGTQ problem there. Many times, that framework erases what happens to people who are subject to all of these things. This framework also enables us to theorize (racial) discrimination in a more complex way than in binaries of when race, ethnicity, legal status, and gender form a representation which leads to possible discrimination by authorities and the uninformed public and other key axes of identity (Nash 2008). Intersectionality does not just refer to personal identity and representation but also leads to structural and systemic discrimination and societal inequalities (Coaston 2019). Intersectionality and othering are useful tools to analyze immigration measures and broader migration issues. Immigration policies and attitudes towards migrants are inherently based on inclusion and exclusion (Jordan & Düvel 2003; Smith 2016) and often intersect with race (Whites are preferred), age (children are vulnerable and deserve assistance), and gender (women too are thought to be more deserving of help than men).

## The racialized other

Standing at 1,400 people, Nigerians are a minuscule minority in Bangkok, but are very visible because of the color of their skin, distinct phenotypical features, and cultural traits (see Issa, this volume). As such, Nigerians are othered because they do not fit in within the norms of Thai society, which has virtually no Black people.

The type of racism Nigerian migrants experience in Thailand is classified as Afrophobia, targeting people from Africa (European Commission 2018). Afrophobia is quite common in many parts of Asia where contemporary racial thinking is informed by historical ways of imagining 'otherness' (see Castillo 2016; Adibe 2017). Afrophobia refers to a range of negative attitudes and feelings towards Black people. It is based on an irrational fear of Black people as 'others,' resulting in antipathy, contempt, and aversion.

Afrophobia includes attitudes, prejudices, and behaviors that exclude and degrade Africans based on the perception that they are outsiders or foreigners who do not belong to Thai society.

Mr. Oke, one of our case study subjects, described his experience of being a racialized other as follows: 'Because we are Black and African, even the garments we sell are often seen as inferior by most Thais despite the fact that we source the materials and design them here.' Mr. Oke indicated that African migrants are perceived as 'lacking skills,' 'selling cheap and inferior items,' and 'engaging in illicit activities.' In order to counter this image of Nigerians, the Nigerian Embassy in Bangkok brought together a group of Nigerian professionals and business owners to form an umbrella organization called Nigeria in Diaspora Organization (NIDO). The group has been tasked with facilitating acquisition of relevant technical skills to enhance the socioeconomic advancement of Nigerians living and working in Thailand (Embassy of Nigeria in Bangkok 2015).

Mr. Mike, another trader, told us that his Thai neighbors do not think he belongs in the neighborhood even though he has been living in Thailand for twelve years. 'Some people still look at me and call me Negro, *Phi dam* (black ghost), *Kee dam* (black shit), and sometimes laugh at me for no apparent reasons.' Mr. Mike thinks that these racial slurs indicate his Thai neighbors' sense of superiority and are expressions of Afrophobia.

Mrs. Nit and Mrs. Tuk are two Thai women who do business with Nigerian traders in the Pratunam area. They said that Nigerians are perceived as *an-ta-rāi* (dangerous) and *na-kląw* (scary). Mr. Oke narrated his experiences with a Thai landlord who evicted him, increased his rent, and refused to help him fill forms needed by the immigration authorities, because the neighbors were afraid of Mr. Oke. In order to appease his Thai tenants, the landlord evicted Mr. Oke. Mr. Oke and Mr. Mike also added that certain hotels and guesthouses refuse to accept Nigerian customers even when there are vacancies.

This irrational fear of Black Nigerians affects Nigerian businesses. Mr. Olu, Mr. Igwe, and Mr. Adele, owners of a cargo business, told us that since the crackdown on African-owned businesses in 2018, they now manage to load only one fourteen-foot container a month, instead of one per week as they used to before 2018. Mr. Olu remarked that discrimination and constant police surveillance put African businesses under a cloud. Even 'Thai banks suspect Nigerians of being criminals,' he said. Given this situation, Nigerians began to use informal channels to remit money. Evidence shows that other migrant communities also resort to the use of informal brokers due to the high hidden costs and paperwork requirements (Kubo 2015; Jampaklay and Kittisuksathit 2009).

Discriminatory practices have forced some businesses to close. In 2019, over ten Nigerian businesses in the Sukhumvit Soi 3 area of Bangkok had to close down due to constant harassment of their African customers and indiscriminate searches of business premises by Thai police and immigration officials. Currently, Nigerian businesses in Pratunam and Silom areas are experiencing similar harassment, and the few surviving enterprises continue to struggle. These stories correspond with Foucault's (1970) understanding of 'othering' as the creation and maintenance of imaginary knowledge of the Other, which comprises cultural representations in service to socio-political power and the establishment of hierarchies of domination.

Despite numerous examples of discrimination and othering of Nigerian migrants, Thais deny this reality. Law enforcement contests their occurrence (Lewis 2014; Nwabueze 2017) and local media attribute expressions of xenophobia against Nigerians to lack of familiarity with migrants from Africa (Rojanaphruk 2020).

## The illegal and criminal other

The traders in our study came to Thailand with the intention of setting up small enterprises. The Immigration Act of 1979 includes investment and long-stay visa provisions meant to attract large-scale foreign investors (Chantavanich, this volume). Small and medium-size entrepreneurs are not eligible to apply for investment visas. As a result, they have few options. However, they can establish legal businesses with Thai business partners or Thai spouses.

Most Nigerians come to Thailand on a tourist visa. Many continue to extend these visas to remain in the country legally, but some overstay and become illegal migrants (Unor 2017). Those who overstay their visas are at the mercy of immigration authorities and are targets of police raids. This situation contributes to the widespread perception that all Nigerians violate immigration laws.

The perception of illegality also extends to the notion that Nigerian businesses operate illegally, while in fact most Nigerian businesses are legally registered in Thailand. This does not stop the police from searching Nigerian business premises and homes with or without search warrants. Mr. Chukwu remarked: 'They [the police] always come in groups, armed to their teeth as if we were terrorists. This creates distrust and fear in the Thai communities and scares customers.' Mr. Oke said: 'I don't really blame them because police harassment and intimidation around our business premises often make Thai people fear being tagged as criminals or people who patronize criminals.'

Ms. Sue, a Nigerian, and Ms. Jen, a Librarian, who work as brokers for clients in Africa, also talked about discriminatory practices against African businesses. Police harassment apparently forced many of their clients to move their businesses to China. Ms. Jen added: 'Coming to eat at an African restaurant is a risk because if the police arrest you, nobody will believe your story, including embassy officials.' According to Mr. Igwe and Mr. Adele, two businessmen involved in the cargo industry, lack of access to the primary and secondary economic sector coupled with discriminatory practices have pushed more vulnerable Nigerians into the underground economy.

Several of our interlocutors said they were dismayed by the public misconception that consistently projects illegality on all Nigerian migrants and thinks that all Nigerians are drug traffickers, internet romance scammers, and illegal migrants. Frustrated, Mr. Oke said the opposite is true. 'We are trying to do everything by the book to be able to take care of our families and Thai wives, but the Thai public often don't see anything good in us.' Mr. Boy, a Thai trader dealing with Africans and Nigerian business persons in Pratunam said: 'Nigerian traders used to come with huge amounts of US dollars and business was good … But because of the strict immigration regulations, we do not see them again.'

Representatives of the general public are not the only people who display negative attitudes towards Nigerians. Staff of different government agencies, especially the labor department, law enforcement, and immigration authorities promulgate similar discourses at the intersection of race, illegality, and criminality. Media publish reports about violence in the African community and attribute predisposition to crime to African migrants (Patin 2012; Agbakuru 2011; ASEAN Now 2017; Draper 2016). Mainstream media stories about Blacks often reinforce racial stereotypes about Black men as 'predators': part of an inferior and criminal subculture (Welch 2007). Here, illegality and criminality intersect with race and make another aspect of Nigerian othering.

## The male other

Perceptions of Black males as criminals are widespread in many parts of the world. In the United States, African American men are often portrayed by the media as 'criminal and dangerous' (Oliver 2003; Colburn & Meander 2018). During 'refugee crises,' 'foreign masculinity' has been used to portray migrants and refugees as a threat to society, to delegitimize solidarity with them, and to argue for restrictive admission measures. In critical masculinity studies, patriarchal gender relations are not exclusively articulated as the structural domination of men over women, but also in hierarchical relations between men or masculinities (e.g., Connell & Messerschmidt 2005; Hearn 2000). While male domination is structured around normative masculine ideals, it is also fundamentally based on the marginalization and exclusion of masculinities that are deemed problematic (Scheibelhofer

2017). When problematic masculinity – be it 'uncivilized,' 'diseased,' or 'asocial' – is ascribed to certain men, the process of othering facilitates their social exclusion, discrimination, and violence against them (Mosse 1996). Problematically different masculinities are hierarchized along the norms of heterosexuality, class relations, race and ethnicity, and citizenship status (Scheibelhofer 2017). Thai authorities and many members of the larger society see Nigerian masculinities as problematic: the protagonists of our study are both racially and ethnically distant from the Thai people; they are also perceived as lacking appropriate immigration status, and not deserving of citizenship.

The othering of migrants, especially male migrants, is now a mainstay of global political and public discourses. During the 2015 'refugee crisis' in Europe, both policy-makers and conservative members of the general public saw the Syrian male refugees as a threat to the security of the European continent and to the Christian identity of the predominantly secular European societies (see Goździak & Márton 2018; Goździak 2021). Othering male migrants goes hand in hand with the debates about deserving refugees and undeserving asylum seekers (Marchetti 2020). While the protagonists of this chapter are neither refugees nor asylum seekers, they are often perceived as criminals illegally residing in Thailand and therefore not deserving to be members of what Anderson calls 'communities of value' imagined and socially constructed as communities populated by 'good citizens, law-abiding and hard-working members of stable and respectable families' (Anderson 2013, 3).

Our research suggests that Nigerian males are not perceived by the Thai authorities and the general public as deserving membership in the communities of value. Nigerians are often portrayed as having values that are not commensurate with the values shared by the predominantly Buddhist Thai society. Duncan McCargo (2009, 2004) contests the assumptions posited by some scholars who suggest that Buddhism is a peaceful religion and that Thailand is a tolerant country guided by the exercise of *metta* (loving-kindness) and characterized by religious freedom (Keyes 1999; Swearer 1995, 1999). The Nigerians in Bangkok are either Muslim or Christian: they are therefore cultural outsiders (Kitiarsa 2007) and do not fit the Thai ethno-national identity.

Intermarriage of Black Nigerians with Thai women is another example of associating Nigerian men with criminality. White husbands are considered rich (Jack 2021), but Black men are equated with poverty and inferiority. Therefore, Nigerian men are not valued as much, even when they are resourceful and possess financial assets. Mr. Oke argued that Caucasian men married to Thai women have no problem extending their visas, while Nigerians married to Thai women encounter many bureaucratic difficulties.

According to Mr. Oke, Nigerians married to Thais are considered insiders; more so than African men not married to Thai women. However, while these masculine subjectivities might position Nigerians married to Thais as cultural insiders, the men continue to be othered.

When several fraudulent marriages of convenience were discovered in the Nigerian community, the news media immediately picked up those stories. Those guilty of 'romance scams' were deported. According to Mr. Chukwu, '[m]ost Nigerians with legitimate marriage visas were also forced to go home for no apparent reasons other than they have lived in Thailand for long periods of time without visiting home.' Mr. Mike's wife indicated that this kind of discrimination intersects with the masculine criminal identity narrative; she has never experienced such an ordeal, despite being in Thailand for a long time without visiting Nigeria.

The process of othering and resulting stereotypes portray male Nigerians as criminals, especially drug dealers. Although they are not the biggest group of drug smugglers in Thailand, local authorities treat them with suspicion (Chantavanich, this volume). Masculinity, intersecting with race, illegality, and criminality, is the main element of othering. It is all about 'being a Black male.'

## Coping strategies

Nigerians are very resilient and have developed several strategies to cope with the adversity of being othered, marginalized, and discriminated against. Marriage with a Thai partner is one such strategy. While there are no official data on the number of marriages between Nigerians and Thais, anecdotal information indicates that the number is significant. Unfortunately, media reports revealed that some of these marriages were contract marriages (Bangkok Post 2018; Thaiger 2019). In 2017, the Thai police arrested seven Nigerian men in possession of 100 fraudulent marriage visas (Nwanne 2017).

Marrying into a Thai family provides a ready-made social network and helps with third party business registration. Mr. Oke estimated that over 80 percent of African businessmen register their businesses in their wife's names. According to Mr. Oke, a Nigerian married to a Thai woman, Nigerian men prefer Thai women because they find them respectful and obedient.

The pattern of Nigerian businessmen marrying Thai women mirrors the behavior of African businessmen living in China. For these men, a union with a Chinese woman comes with advantages that include a relatively easy way of obtaining a legal status, an ability to access reliable Chinese suppliers, and an opportunity to build strong business networks in China. Ado and colleagues showed that Nigerians who married Chinese women attribute their success in China to their Chinese wives. Their integration strategies include learning Chinese to communicate with their Chinese counterparts, adopting Chinese values, cultural traits, and ways of doing business (Ado et al. 2016).

Another strategy used by Nigerian businessmen is to hire Thai staff to fend off police harassment of African shopkeepers and to appease Thai customers who mistrust Nigerian business owners and do not like to patronize African businesses even when they sell unique products. This is an effective practice in running African shops. However, this strategy does not facilitate business expansion beyond the small African enclave. Few Thais patronize African shops and even fewer have ever been to an African restaurant. Thai people have limited contact with African culture and cuisine. Given this lack of interest in African products and services, many Nigerian business owners cater predominantly to African customers, both those living in Thailand and those visitors from Africa.

While Thai customers are reluctant to patronize Nigerian businesses, this niche economy attracts Middle Eastern customers and more recently also Vietnamese, Cambodians, and Burmese. This clientele helps the African-owned businesses economically, but the migrant customers attract immigration raids because these groups of migrants suffer similar prejudices that befall Nigerians.

Attempts to integrate into the Thai society constitute another coping strategy. Some of our interlocutors enrolled in different courses of study at Thai institutions of higher education or started learning the Thai language. Many Nigerians we spoke with believe that speaking Thai makes it easier to do business, deal with the in-laws, and the Thai public at large. Ms. Sue enrolled in a Thai language course at a language school owned by a Nigerian. Unfortunately, the presence of Nigerians in the school makes it an object of constant police harassment. In addition, African graduates of Thai universities might eventually face many obstacles trying to enter the labor market in Thailand.

Integration attempts may not always be successful. Ms. Sue indicated that despite her business connections and years of interactions with Thais, she has not gained much respect from her Thai customers. Ms. Sue has chosen invisibility as a strategy. She avoids coming to Pratunam during peak business hours because of racially motivated discrimination. Instead, she focuses on serving Africans. She also lightens her skin, builds alliances with her own compatriots, and creates connections with Thai and Nigerian security agencies, and faith-based self-help organizations. She tries to remain invisible by marketing and selling her products online (Issa, this volume).

African entrepreneurs have developed some strategies to deal with corruption. Ms. Jen revealed that friendly relationships with Thai agencies help to shield Africans from harassment by security officers or immigration authorities. In order to maintain friendly relationships, Africans bribe them or collaborate with them in some ways. According to Mr. Chukwu, some Nigerians spy on fellow compatriots and report their activities to the immigration officials in exchange for protection. Mr. Chukwu narrated his own experience with needing to bribe someone as follows:

> I was once forced to pay over 200,000 baht to a Thai person on account that a customer who scammed the lady used the same account to pay me for the products he bought from me. To avoid problems with the police, my Thai wife pled with me to pay the money. I did, but after that I hired a reputable Thai lawyer to prove my innocence. When the lawyer contacted the police, they refunded the money, closed the case, and apologized.

While some African entrepreneurs condone bribing public officials to keep their businesses safe, these activities put African migrants at the intersection of illegality. Hiah (2020) revealed that 'normalization of corruption' is better understood by the extent to which public officials depend on kickbacks to survive.

## Conclusions

In this exploratory study, we identified numerous examples of discrimination against Nigerian migrants at the intersection of race, il/legality, and masculinity. Our interlocutors provided accounts of both verbal and nonverbal acts of discrimination steeped in structural and systemic racism that permeates all aspects of Nigerian migrants' lives in Bangkok. These acts of othering cannot be excused by the Thai society's lack of familiarity and exposure to African migrants and the nonexistence of research on the African diaspora in Thailand.

Our findings confirm the original hypothesis that Nigerians in Thailand are othered. The process of othering subjects them to systemic oppression and economic vulnerability at the intersectionality of race (being Black), illegality (visa overstay and engagement in drug smuggling), and masculinity. These findings are largely acknowledged by the host communities (Colbey 2018; UCA News 2020a, 2020b), Nigerian businesspersons, and human rights agencies (Bohwongprasert & Rithdee 2018; Ehrlich 2020; Saksornchai 2018) as well as researchers (Lewis 2014; Nwabueze 2017; Chantavanich, this volume). Therefore, to overcome the discrimination and stereotyping of Nigerians and to promote better understanding and structural cooperation towards a more inclusive society, we recommend the following.

First, there is a need for public campaigns to address media over-representation of Nigerians (and other Africans) in Thailand as dangerous and criminal. The media ought to be encouraged to publish human interest stories about Nigerian immigrants to provide the Thai citizens with a more intimate portrait of the Nigerian diaspora and the challenges they face. The Thai government should join forces with the Nigerian Embassy in Bangkok, the Asiafrica Foundation (ASAFO), and the Thai-Africa Partnership for Sustainable Development (TAPSD) founded in 2017 to present a realistic picture of the Nigerian diaspora (Chantavanich, this volume).

Second, the Thai Ministry of Foreign Affairs needs to work with Thai embassies in Africa to treat African visa applicants without prejudice. Such prejudice may come from a high number of African overstayers. In 2015, 800,000 people overstayed their visa in Thailand; the majority from Africa, India, and Bangladesh. Consequently, the Immigration Bureau proposed a heavier punishment and a re-entry ban on overstayers (Bangkok Post 2015). The new measures make the application process more complicated and demanding to prevent fraud similar to that discovered in Abuja (Royal Thai Embassy Abuja 2020). While the strict requirements can be interpreted as prejudice, the rules and regulations need to be carefully explained to Nigerian visa applicants. In the long run, it will protect them from abuse by unscrupulous scammers.

Third, Nigerian businessmen in Thailand should be able to conduct business legally in the country without being discriminated against. Thai policy-makers and politicians should consider South–South Cooperation with Nigeria, particularly for small and medium-size entrepreneurs, to reflect their deepening diplomatic, economic, and bilateral trade interests. Currently, the Thai government has utilized the promotion of small and medium-sized enterprises as a means of achieving sustained and healthy economic growth locally (Turner et al 2016). Extending this strategy to Nigerian businesses would be a positive step in the right direction, but it would require considerable lobbying efforts on the part of both Nigerians and the wider African diaspora. Nigerian business owners need to decide whether they want to operate small scale businesses in the niche economy and continue circular migration patterns or strive to formalize their business efforts. Additionally, Thailand should consider using the African Continental Free Trade Area (AfCFTA) (Abimbola 2021) to expand its trade relationships with more African countries. This would be economically advantageous to all partners and would improve the Thai public's perception of Africans.

Fourth, longer-term transformation of Thai–Nigerian relations requires an improved mutual understanding. The younger generation of African

Thais (born out of intermarriages between Nigerian men and Thai women) has a role to play in this arena. Several African Thais become successful in the entertainment industry in Thailand. A Malian–Thai actress shared her past experience of being discriminated against and bullied at school. A university lecturer suggested that her narrative was more impactful than anti-discrimination laws. The narrative might be useful in raising awareness, but strong anti-discrimination laws give Africans a legal recourse. Some scholars suggest that Thais' discrimination against Black people is rooted in ignorance, rather than hatred as we are seeing in the United States, for example. Racial prejudice from ignorance can be rectified more easily than deeply ingrained racism (Thaitrakulpanich 2020). Another black African Thai actor also said he hopes to see more roles for African Thais in the entertainment industry (Rojanaphruk 2020). These examples come from African Thais who grew up in Thailand and are not newcomers like the Nigerian migrants. However, these statements are encouraging as they reflect the changing attitudes towards Black people among Thai youth. On the Nigerian side, attempts to learn Thai language, study in Thai schools and colleges can facilitate integration. Also, presenting themselves in a manner that distances Nigerian migrants from illegality and crime will bring about a new perception and, hopefully, lead to public acceptance. These changes will certainly take time.

# References

Abimbola, Olumide. 2021. *Africa's Free-Trade Area Signals Intent for a New Kind of Relationship with the EU*. Brussels: European Union, Heinrich Boll Stiftung. Available at: https://eu.boell.org/en/2021/05/19/africas-free-trade-area-signals-intent-new-kind-relationship-eu.

Adibe, Jideofor. 2017. "Impact of Xenophobic Attacks Against Africans in India on Afro-India Relations." *Journal of African Foreign Affairs* 4(1–2): 85–98.

Ado, Abdoulkadre, Elli Chrysostome and Su Zhan. 2016. "Examining Adaptation Strategies of Sub-Saharan African Immigrant Entrepreneurs in China: The Case of Guangdong." *Journal of Developmental Entrepreneurship* 21(4).

Agbakuru, Johnbosco. 2011. "Nigeria: 700 Citizens in Thai Prisons, Others Dead." *All Africa*, October 5. Available at: https://allafrica.com/stories/201110050817.html.

Anderson, Bridget. 2013. *Us and Them? The Dangerous Politics of Immigration Control*. Oxford: Oxford University Press.

ASEAN Now. 2017. "Massive Raid as 'Coloreds' Targeted in Nana This Morning." September 16. Available at: https://aseannow.com/topic/1002502-massive-raid-as-coloreds-targeted-in-nana-this-morning/.

Bangkok Post. 2018. "5 Nigerians, 12 Thais Held in Romance Scams." *Bangkok Post*, September 15. Available at: https://www.bangkokpost.com/thailand/general/1540570/5-nigerians-12-thais-held-in-romance-scams.

Bangkok Post. 2015. "Overstayers Face Stiff Re-Entry Bans: PM Mulls Request to Use Special Powers." *Bangkok Post*, October 26 Available at: https://www.bangkokpost.com/thailand/general/742528/overstayers-face-stiff-re-entry-bans.

BBC. 2016. "Racist Thailand Skin-Whitening Advert Is Withdrawn." *BBC News*, January 8. Available at: https://www.bbc.com/news/world-asia-35261748.

Beauvoir, Simone de. 1952. *The Second Sex*. New York: Alfred Knopf.

Bohwongprasert, Yvonne and Kong Rithdee. 2018. "Out of Africa." *Bangkok Post*, March 5. Available at: https://www.bangkokpost.com/life/social-and-lifestyle/1422527/out-of-africa.

Castillo, Roberto. 2016. "Of Washing Powder, Afrophobia and Racism in China." *The Conversation*, August 11. Available at: https://theconversation.com/of-washing-powder-afrophobia-and-racism-in-china-60274.

Clifford, Jake. 2020. "Cross River Born Ettah Emmanuel Bags 2020 IESA Award in Thailand." *Wee Talk Naija*, January 26. Available at: https://weetalknaija.com.ng/news/breaking-and-latest-metro-news-in-nigeria-news-events-and-happenings-in-iesa.html.

Coaston, Jane. 2019. "The Intersectionality Wars: When Kimberlé Crenshaw Coined the Term 30 Years Ago, It Was a Relatively Obscure Legal Concept. Then It Went Viral." *Vox*, May 20.

Colbey, Adele. 2018. "Arbitrary Arrests Make Life in Bangkok Hell for African Migrants." *Prachatai English*, June 20. Available at: https://prachatai.com/english.

Colburn, Alayna and Lisa A. Melamder. 2018. "Beyond Black and White: An Analysis of Newspaper Representations of Alleged Criminal Offenders Based on Race and Ethnicity." *Journal of Contemporary Criminal Justice* 34(4): 383–398. https://doi.org/10.1177/104398621878773.

Connell, R. W. and James W. Messerschmidt. 2005. "Hegemonic Masculinity: Rethinking the Concept." *Gender & Society* 19(6): 829–859.

Crenshaw, Kimberle. 1991. "Mapping the Margins: Intersectionality, Identity Politics, and Violence against Women of Color." *Stanford Law Review* 43(6): 1241–1299.

Draper, John. 2016. "Darkies Are Ugly," *Prachatai*, January 9. Available at: https://prachatai.com/english/node/5755.

Duncan, J. 1993. "Sites of Representation: Place, Time and the Discourse of the Other." In: *Representing Cultural Geography*, edited by James S. Duncan and David Ley. London: Routledge.

Embassy of Nigeria in Bangkok. 2015. *Our Stewardship Democracy*. Bangkok: Amarin Printing and Publishing PLC.

Erlich, Richard S. 2020. "Racism and Black Lives Matter in Thailand." *Scoop Independent News*, June 25. Available at: https://www.scoop.co.nz/stories/HL2006/S00185/racism-black-lives-matter-in-thailand.htm.

Eromosele, Diana Ozemebhoya. 2015. "Being Black in Thailand: We're Treated Better Than Africans, and Boy Do We Hate It." *The Root*, May 26. Available at: https://www.theroot.com/being-black-in-thailand-we-re-treated-better-than-afri-1790859954.

European Commission. 2018. *Afrophobia: Acknowledging and Understanding the Challenges to Ensure Effective Responses*. Brussels: European Commission.

Ewubare, Kess. 2021. "Nigerian Lecturer Makes Country Proud, Emerges Overall Best PhD Student in Thailand." *Legit*, May 2. Available at: https://www.legit.ng /1414101-nigerian-lecturer-country-proud-emerges-student-thailand.html.

Fanon, Franz. 1963. *Black Skin, White Masks*. Harmondsworth: Penguin.

Fernquest, Jon. 2012a. "Prince Mahidol Awards 2012. Brit, Nigerian Win Mahidol Awards." *Bangkok Post*, November 22. Available at: https://www.bangkokpost .com/learning/advanced/322768/prince-mahidol-awards-2012.

Fernquest, Jon. 2012b. "Thailand's Police Corruption Problem." *Bangkok Post*, December 24. Available at: https://www.bangkokpost.com/learning/advanced /327755/thailand-police-corruption-problem.

Foucault, Michel. 1970. *The Order of Things: An Archaeology of the Human Sciences*. Sheridan: Random House.

Goździak, Elżbieta M. and Péter Márton. 2018. "Where the Wild Things Are: Fear of Islam and the Anti-refugee Rhetoric in Hungary and in Poland." *Central and Eastern European Migration Review* 7(2): 125–151. https://doi.org/10.17467/ ceeMr2018.04.

Goździak, Elżbieta M. 2021. *Human Trafficking as a New (In)Security Threat*. New York: Palgrave.

Grant-Thomas, Andrew. 2016. "Editor's Introduction." *Othering and Belonging* 1: 10–12.

Gye, Hugo. 2013. "Map Shows World's Most Racist Countries." *Daily Mail*, May 16. Available at: https://www.dailymail.co.uk/news/article-2325502/Map-shows -worldsracist-countries-answers-surprise-you.html.

Hearn, Jeff. 2000. "Is Masculinity Dead? A Critique of the Concept of Masculinity/ Masculinities." In: *Understanding Masculinities*, edited by Mairtin Mac An Ghaill, pp. 202–217. Buckingham: Open University Press.

Hiah, Jing. 2020. "The Client Side of Everyday Corruption in Central and Eastern Europe: The Case of Chinese Migrant Entrepreneurs in Romania." *European Journal of Criminology* 17(6): 877–895. https://doi.org/10.1177/1477370819830296.

Jack, Albert. 2021. "The Reason Thai Women Love Foreign Men." *Bangkok Jack*, January 4. Available at: https://bangkokjack.com/2021/01/04/thai-women-love -foreign-men/.

Jampaklay, Aree and Sirinam Kittisuksathi. 2009. *Migrant Workers' Remittances: Cambodia, Lao PDR and Myanmar*. Bangkok: ILO.

Jordan, Bill and Frank Düvell. 2003. *Irregular Migration: The Dilemmas of Transnational Mobility*. Cheltenham: Edward Elgar Pub.

Judd, Adam. 2018. "Thai Police Announce All Nigerians in Thailand Will Be Investigated." *The Pattaya News*, August 10. Available at: https://thepattayanews .com/2018/08/10/thai-police-announce-all-nigerians-in-thailand-will-be -investigated/.

Kalu, K. 2007. "Migration and Institution Building in Africa: Lessons from the Lagos Plan of Action." In: *Population Movements, Conflicts and Displacements in Nigeria*, edited by Toin Falola and O. O. Okpeh Ochai Okpeh, pp. 133–153. Asmara, Eritrea: Africa World Press.

Keyes, Charles F. 1999. "Buddhist Politics and Their Revolutionary Origins in Thailand." *International Political Science Review* 10(2): 121–142.

Kerrison, Erin, Jennifer Cobbina and Kimberly Bender. 2018. "Stop-Gaps, Lip Service, and the Perceived Futility of Body-Worn Police Officer Cameras in Baltimore City." *Journal of Ethnic & Cultural Diversity in Social Work* 27(3): 271–288. https://doi.org/10.1080/15313204.2018.1479912

Kitiarsa, Pattana. 2007. "Muai Thai Cinema and the Burdens of Thai Men." *South East Asia Research* 15(3): 407–424.

Kluckhohn, Richard (Ed.). 1962. *Culture and Behavior: Collected Essays of Clyde Kluckhohn.* New York: The Free Press of Glencoe, Inc.

Kubo, Koji. 2015. "Evolving Informal Remittance Methods of Myanmar Migrant Workers in Thailand." *ERIA Discussion Paper Series.* Available at: https://www.eria.org/ERIA-DP-2015-45.pdf.

Lewis, Melinda. 2014. "Being Black in Thailand." *Chiangmai City Life*, January 30. https://www.chiangmaicitylife.com/clg/our-city/opinion/being-black-in-thailand/.

Marchetti, Chiara. 2020. (Un)Deserving refugees Contested access to the 'community of value' in Italy In *Europe and the Refugee Response: A Crisis of Values?* Edited By Elżbieta M. Goździak, Izabella Main, Brigitte Suter, pp. 236–252.

McCargo, Duncan. 2004. "Buddhism, Democracy and Identity in Thailand." *Democratization ResearchGate* 11(4): 155–170. https://doi.org/10.1080/1351034042000234576.

McCargo, Duncan. 2009. "The Politics of Buddhist Identity in Thailand's Deep South: The Demise of Civic Religion?" *Journal of Southeast Asian Studies* 40(1): 11–32.

Mosse, George L. 1996. *The Image of Man: The Creation of Modern Masculinity.* New York: Oxford University Press.

Nash, Jennifer C. 2008. "Re-Thinking Intersectionality." *Feminist Review* 89(1): 1–15.

Nwabueze, Tony. 2017. *A Public Opinion on the Effect of Language Barrier on Racial Assimilation.* Master Thesis. Bangkok: Siam University.

Nwanne, Tony. 2017. "Seven Nigerians Arrested with 100 Visas in Thailand." *News Break*, June 22. Available at: https://newsbreak.ng/seven-nigerians-arrested-100-visas-thailand/.

OECD/ILO. 2017. *How Immigrants Contribute to Thailand's Economy.* Available at: 10.1787/9789264287747-en.

Oliver, Mary Beth. 2003. "African American Men as "Criminal and Dangerous": Implications of Media Portrayals of Crime on the "Criminalization" of African American Men." *Journal of African American Studies* 7(2): 3–18.

Patin, Jennifer L. 2012. "Nigerians in Thailand: Two Sides to Every Story." *Thailand Law Forum*, July 5, 2012. Available at: http://www.thailawforum.com/Nigerians-In-Thailand.html.

Rojanaphruk, Pravit. 2020. "Opinion: From American Racism to Thai Chauvinism." *Khaosod News*, June 7.

Royal Thai Embassy Abuja. 2020. "Royal Thai Embassy Abuja Visa Regulations." *Ministry of Foreign Affairs*, March 4. Available at: https://image.mfa.go.th/mfa/0/xPBEVeSDJi/visa.pdf.

Said, Edward W. 2016. *Orientalism: Western Conceptions of the Orient.* Camberwell: Penguin Books.

Sakaowan, Prae and Todd Ruiz. 2014. "60 Thai Superstitious Dos and Don'ts for Your Convenience." *Coconuts Bangkok*, February 6. https://coconuts.co/ bangkok/news/60-thai-superstitious-dos-and-donts-your-convenience/.

Saksornchai, Jintamas. 2018. "Police to Investigate 'All Nigerians' in Thailand." *Khaosod English*, August 10, 2018. Available at: https://www.khaosodenglish .com/featured/2018/08/10/police-to-investigate-all-nigerians-in-thailand/.

Scheibelhofer, Paul. 2017. "It Won't Work Without Ugly Pictures': Images of Othered Masculinities and the Legitimization of Restrictive Refugee Politics in Austria." *NORMA* 12(2): 96–111. https://doi.org/10.1080/18902138.2017.1341222.

Sibley, David. 2007. *Geographies of Exclusion: Society and Difference in the West.* London: Routledge.

Smith, Ben. 2016. "Intersectional Discrimination and Substantive Equality: A Comparative and Theoretical Perspective." *The Equal Rights Review* 16: 73–102.

Staszak, Jean-François. 2008. "Other/Otherness." In: *International Encyclopedia of Human Geography*, edited by Rob Kitchin and Nigel Thrift, pp. 43–47. Oxford: Elsevier.

Swearer, Donald K. 1995. *The Buddhist World of Southeast Asia.* Albany, NY: SUNY Press.

Swearer, Donald K. 1999. "Centre and Periphery: Buddhism and Politics in Modern Thailand." In: *Buddhism and Politics in Twentieth Century Asia*, edited by Ian Harris, pp. 194–228. London: Continuum.

Thaiger. 2019. "Nigerian and Thai Wife Arrested in Chon Buri over $50,000 Romance Scam." *The Thaiger*, July 7, 2019. Available at: https://thethaiger.com/hot-news /crime/nigerian-and-thai-wife-arrested-in-chon-buri-over-50000-romance-scam.

Thaitrakulpanich, Asaree. 2020. "Straight Outta Bangkok: What It's Like to Be a Nigerian Rapper in Thailand." *Khaosod English*, July 8. Available at: https:// www.khaosodenglish.com/life/arts/2020/07/08/straight-outta-bangkok-what-its -like-to-be-a-nigerian-rapper-in-thailand/.

Titapiwatanakun, Boonjit and Boosaree Titapiwatanakun. 2012. *Support for the Association of Southeast Asian Nations Plus Three. Integrated Food Security Framework. The Rice Situation in Thailand.* Bangkok: Kasetsart University.

Turner, Mark, Sineenat Sermcheep, Sekasan Anantasirijkiat and Piti Srisangnam. 2016. "Small and Medium-Sized Enterprises in Thailand: Government Policy and Economic Development." *Asia Pacific Journal of Public Administration* 38(4): 251–269. https://doi.org/10.1080/23276665.2016.1256545.

Udah, Hyacinth. 2019. "Searching for a Place to Belong in a Time of Othering." *Social Sciences* 11(11): 297. https://doi.org/10.3390/socsci8110297.

Unor, Anthony U. 2017. "Nigerian Drugs Syndicates in Thailand: A Panacea for the Mayhem." The 12th Graduate Study Presentation Conference. Rangsit University.

Union of Catholic Asian (UCA) News Reporter. 2020a. "Thailand. Thai Woman Highlights Racism in her Homeland. Social Media Star Blames Ingrained Prejudices on Thailand's Dominant Beauty Industry and Television Shows." UCA News Bangkok, June. Available at: https://www.ucanews.com/news/thai -woman-highlights-racism-in-her-homeland/88426.

UCA News Reporter. 2020b. "Thailand. African Priest Hits a Wall of Prejudice in Thailand. Missionary Has Even Faced Racial Discrimination from Fellow Catholics in the Kingdom." UCA News Bangkok, June 21. Available at: https://www.ucanews.com/news/african-priest-hits-a-wall-of-prejudice-in-thailand/88469#.

Welch, Kelly. 2007. "Black Criminal Stereotypes and Racial Profiling." *Journal of Contemporary Criminal Justice* 23(3): 276–288. https://doi.org/10.1177/1043986207306870.

World Bank. 2015. "Malaysia Economic Monitor: Immigrant Labor." Kuala Lumpur. Available at: http://documents.worldbank.org/curated/en/753511468197095162/Malaysia-Economic-monitor-immigrantlabor.

# 7 African gems traders in Chanthaburi province

## Premjai Vungsiriphisal

### Chanthaburi, a global gems market

There are virtually no studies of African communities in Thailand. In this chapter, I present the community of African gems and precious stones traders who settled in Chanthaburi Province in southeast Thailand.

The discovery of the sapphire deposit near Pailin (now in Cambodia) in the 19th century transformed Chanthaburi into an important center of Thailand's gems and jewelry industry. Chanthaburi produced world-class rubies and blue, yellow, and black star sapphires (Crawfurd 1828; Pallegoix 1854, cited in Hughes 2010). With the loss of Pailin in 1907 to French Indochina (and then Cambodia), the mining and gem trading activity in the region decreased considerably (Smyth 1898). Furthermore, haphazard excavation of rough gemstones from 1962 onwards resulted in a significant decline in the volume of gems in Chanthaburi (Hughes 2010). When modern machinery replaced manual digging, Khao Ploy Waen (The Hill of Gems), the main mine in Chanthaburi, was further depleted (Duggleby 2014). Thai traders started exploring new sources of precious stones in neighboring countries: Myanmar, Cambodia, Vietnam, and Australia. Later on, Thai traders looked towards East Africa – Madagascar, Tanzania, and Mozambique – where gems have been mined since 1993 (Pardieu 2019).

Starting in 2016, gems trading by foreign traders was limited in many parts of Africa due to frequent robberies. After 2017, fewer and fewer Thai merchants traveled to Africa to deal directly with African miners. Instead, they started relying on intermediary traders (Hunter & Lawson 2020).

Nowadays, traders from various parts of the world come to Chanthaburi every weekend to buy and sell rough and cut gems. African gemstone traders constitute an important part of this international market (GIA 2015). The number of African traders coming to Chanthaburi has increased exponentially over the past 20 years, from about ten individuals to a community of approximately 700 settlers, including their family members. Over

DOI: 10.4324/9781003286554-7

80 percent of the traders hail from West Africa: Guinea, Mali, and the Ivory Coast. They are important contributors to the vitality of the gems and jewelry industry in Chanthaburi, where some 80 percent of exported gems are cut and quality enhanced. The African gemstone traders have formed a trade association, but the Chanthaburi Gem and Jewelry Traders Association is the face of the gemstone trade in the province and is reluctant to accept African traders as its members.

Historically, Chanthaburi has always been a multicultural province, where Chinese, Vietnamese, and Shan migrants worked and lived alongside native Thais (Hughes 2010). These migrants came to Chanthaburi at different times and all contributed to the development and prosperity of the province. Shan brought their knowledge and skills in gems mining and cutting; Chinese brought ship building expertise (Chantavanich & Triemwittaya 2020), trading, and agricultural know-how, while Vietnamese excelled in mat weaving and fishing (Chetpatanawanich & Reungviset 1995).

Asian migrants have blended into the social and cultural fabric of the province, but Africans seem to be experiencing integration challenges. They integrated into the economy of Chanthaburi, but are not accepted socially and culturally, and experience racism and xenophobia.

## Research process and research questions

I was born and raised in Chanthaburi and have been able to observe the arrival of Africans over many years, but never formally researched any aspect of the community. This study is my first attempt to look more rigorously at African gems traders in my home province. Undertaking this exploratory study, I had to balance my position as an insider, who had seen the development of the multicultural community in Chanthaburi during my school years and witnessed the prosperity of the gemstone industry with my current position of an outsider who has worked for many years in Bangkok, but has been able to observe the arrival of international traders from Africa, new settlers from diverse cultures, and their integration challenges and reactions from the host community.

This chapter is based on 21 in-depth interviews carried out between March 2019 and April 2021. I interviewed two Guinean and one Malian trader to understand the reasons why they came to do business and settle in this area and to analyze their relationships with local residents. I also talked with two representatives of the African Gems Association to better understand the history and the evolution of the association, including networking with local businesses. Since the Africans who settled in Chanthaburi brought with them their spouses and children, I talked with two Guinean parents about their experiences sending children to local schools. All of these interviews were conducted in English and lasted between one and two hours.

Additionally, I interviewed two Thai gems traders, a Thai representative of the local gem association, one civil society member, and three local residents about their attitudes towards the African community, their assessment of the Africans' contribution and integration into the local economy and community. I also talked to a local imam about the integration of Africans into the religious community and the causes of both positive and negative attitudes towards Africans. I interviewed an immigration officer to elicit information on the size, immigration status, and residential patterns of the African population in Chanthaburi. Finally, I spoke to two school administrators and three teachers from two local schools about their challenges and successes in teaching African students. All of these interviews were in Thai.

In addition to individual interviews, I conducted two focus groups with 11 students, ranging in age between 10 and 16 years; four of them were born in Africa and came to Chanthaburi with their families, seven were born in Thailand to African parents. Additionally, I held one focus group with four non-African migrant students and one focus group with five native Thai students. I asked about their attitudes and relationships with their classmates from different countries, teachers' attitudes towards foreign-born students, and discrimination they have faced. These discussions were conducted in schools where children felt most comfortable. Each focus group lasted about one to 1.5 hours. None of the discussions were tape-recorded, but I took copious notes during and immediately after each interview or focus group.

My analysis centers on three issues: settlement, integration, and local response to the arrival of African gemstone traders. Presenting findings stemming from my exploratory study of existing relationships and tensions between the local Thai citizenry and the African newcomers, I try to answer the following research questions: How well do the African migrants integrate into the local community? Why has the presence of Africans raised anxiety among local people? What are the causes of the anxiety? Does the African minority face discrimination? How does their treatment compare with other migrant groups in Chanthaburi? I end the chapter with some reflections on why a small group of gems traders from Africa has caused concern and even fear among the local population. Is it a case of fear of small numbers? (Appadurai 2006).

## Theoretical frameworks

Two concepts are important to my analysis of the settlement of African gems traders in Chanthaburi, namely niche economy/niche migration and migrant integration.

Niche formation is the logical outcome of migration (Waldinger 1996). Alejandro Portes (1994) and Edna Bonacich (1973) emphasize the importance of ethnic bonding and ethnic solidarity in niche formation. The phenomena of niche and enclave economies have often been explained from a 'disadvantage' perspective, referring to migrants' lack of contacts, proficiency in the local language, and discrimination (Schrover 2001). The African traders in Chanthaburi both benefited from the niche economy in Chanthaburi and faced challenges. They have developed beneficial contacts with Thai traders, but faced discrimination, not so much on the basis of inferior skills, but on the basis of race and ethnicity. They have also experienced isolation, mainly because they do not speak Thai and are not motivated to learn it.

I follow Jane Guyer's conceptualization of the term 'niche economy' (Guyer 1997). Of particular importance to my understanding of Africans' participation in the niche economy of gems trading in Chanthaburi is her focus on migration from one market to another, diversification of personal enterprise portfolios, employment and skill, and carving out careers by advancing within or moving among international market niches, including international and transcontinental markets (see also Berry 2004). I also use the term 'niche' more colloquially to denote a specialized segment of the market for a particular kind of product or service.

The term 'integration' represents an evolution in migration scholarship more than any change in the migrant experience. Many of the terms used by migration scholars to describe migrants' construction of their new lives oscillated around the outsider–insider dichotomy. A vocabulary that included such terms as assimilation, acculturation, incorporation, and socioeconomic adjustment seemed 'wedded to a normative vision of societies as culturally homogenous, in which residents born in other places are exceptional, rather than customary participants in economic, social, and cultural life' (Ray 2002).

The term assimilation, which implies a willful departure from the culture of origin, has fallen into disrepute of late. Scholars have increasingly recognized that migrants adapting to new circumstances and societies follow a number of different paths. The growing multiculturalism around the world has questioned the very idea of integration and incentives to integrate (Goździak 2005). The newest trend in migration studies is to look at migrants' adjustment to new circumstances through the lens of belonging, often multiple belongings (Pawlak & Goździak 2019). In this study, I ask whether African gems traders belong in Chanthaburi: Do they belong to the networks of international gems traders? Are they recognized as legitimate citizens of the town? Or are they rejected by the locals?

## Arrival of Africans in Chanthaburi

The first African gemstone traders arrived in Chanthaburi in the early 2000s. At first, a few African traders came as temporary visitors to sell rough gemstones. Once their sales were completed, they returned to Africa. Gradually, the number of African traders became bigger, the period of stay longer, and finally some of the traders decided to settle in the area. Nowadays most immigrant buyers do not go back home to sell precious stones anymore. Colored gemstones such as rubellite, aquamarine, and tourmaline are in high demand in China (Bhattacharya et al. 2017) and the immigrant traders started selling their gems to the Chinese.

In 2021, there were 3,080 trading companies in Chanthaburi. Slightly over ten percent (364) are gemstone companies. The majority (63.5 percent or 231 companies) are owned by or operate in partnership with African traders (Office of Provincial Commercial Affairs Chanthaburi 2021). Among the 680 skilled immigrants registered as gems traders, 620 are Africans, followed by Indians (86), American, British, Malaysian, and Chinese. There are also small numbers of traders from Italy, Myanmar, Pakistan, South Korea, Sri Lanka, Sweden, and Vietnam (Chanthaburi Employment Office 2021).

Almost all African immigrants are involved in gemstone trading; a very small number work as teachers. Estimated at approximately 700 people, including dependents, they constitute the biggest African community in Thailand. Between 2017 and 2019, the majority of Africans in Chanthaburi held business visas (Chanthaburi Immigration Office 2017–19). According to Thailand's immigration policy, foreigners who enter the country as skilled workers or hold business visas are eligible to bring their family members. One third of the visa holders were dependents, mainly from Guinea and Mali.

The presence of family members has made the African community in Chanthaburi more visible. The African women who shop at the local market in their bright clothes, with children in tow, are noticed by local Thais. 'We saw them [*African women*] in their brightly colored clothes. They often come to the market with their children. They have many children, at least two to three. They tie one child around their waist and another child walks behind,' said Da, a 40-year-old Thai woman.

East Africa is a major source of rough gemstones (Pardieu 2019). However, African gemstone traders in Chanthaburi hail mainly from West Africa. According to the Chanthaburi Immigration Bureau, the majority of Africans residing in the province in 2017–2019 come from Guinea (76–80%), followed by Mali (12–14%), Ghana (4–6%), and the Ivory Coast (2.3–5%). Smaller numbers came from Senegal, Togo, and Sierra Leone. A few Africans in Chanthaburi are from South Africa, Mozambique, and Zambia.

This demographic profile mirrors the characteristics of gemstone traders in Bangkok, where Guineans constitute the majority of traders, followed by Nigerians and Sierra Leoneans (Hunter & Lawson 2020). They are intermediaries in the African gemstones trading chain; they buy gemstones from miners in East Africa to sell in Thailand. The Guinean network also brings rubies from Mozambique, which further confirms the role West African networks play in bringing gemstones to Thailand. The Guinean network is increasingly important, especially since 2016, when mining without license in Mozambique became illegal and many foreign buyers stopped buying directly from local miners, but began to rely on West African intermediaries.

The gemstone trading opportunity was the fundamental reason that drove West Africans to settle in Chanthaburi. Affordable cost of living and peaceful atmosphere was an added magnet. 'I started doing business here [*in Chanthaburi*] long time ago. I used to come and go between Africa, Bangkok, and Chanthaburi. I found Chanthaburi cheaper and more peaceful than Bangkok,' said Mohamed, a 45-year-old Guinean trader.

There are no other businesses run by Africans in town. Chanthaburi is an agricultural province that produces various kinds of fruits, spices, and seafood. These products are not easy to export to Africa. Surprisingly, there are also no shops or restaurants owned by Africans despite the fact that most immigrant communities anywhere in the world set up their own stores and eateries to cater to their co-ethnics.

## Integration challenges

Thailand has a long history of immigration and became a net immigration country in the early 1990s (OECD/ILO 2017). In 2019, Thailand hosted approximately 4.9 million non-Thai residents, a substantial increase from 3.7 million in 2014. Thailand benefits significantly from their presence. Migrant workers help fill labor shortages, contribute to economic growth, and are becoming ever more important as Thai society ages. Constituting over ten percent of the total labor force, their work is thought to contribute between 4.3 to 6.6 percent of Thailand's Gross Domestic Product (GDP) (Harkins 2019).

Thai immigration law considers international migration a temporary phenomenon. However, in reality many migrants stay in the country for prolonged periods of time (Huguet et al. 2012). The African gemstones traders are a perfect example of migrants who decided to settle in Chanthaburi.

The perennial question that arises, once migrants settle, is that of integration. While Thailand increasingly relies on immigrant labor, the country does not have an integration policy, and does not consider multiculturalism as a desirable feature of the Thai society. Throughout the 20th century, homogeneity had been incessantly stressed in official discourses as an important part of nation-building. 'Those who do not fit into the narrowly defined "Thai-ness" have therefore been deemed "others" and outsiders, threats to the unity of the homogeneously conceived nation' (Hayami 2006: 283).

Integration is, of course, an extraordinarily complex two-way process, shaped by factors including human and social capital and the characteristics of sending and receiving countries. Below I explore selected facets of economic and cultural integration of African gemstone traders in Chanthaburi.

### Integration into the niche economy

Socio-economic integration has been determined in terms of economic standing relative to the host society, measured by indicators such as education, occupation, and income (Goździak 2005). Analyzing economic integration of African traders in Chanthaburi, we must emphasize a significant characteristic of this community, namely its involvement in a singular economic market of gems trading. This is in contrast to Africans in other countries who work in various kinds of jobs or run different types of businesses.

In China, for example, which hosts the highest number of Africans in Asia, African migrants work in diverse jobs and businesses. Many are exporters who buy all kinds of 'Made in China' products to sell in Africa. In Xiaobei Lu, the heart of Guangzhou's Little Africa, bilingual signs can be seen on shops, restaurants, and halal shops. Researchers have observed interactions between Africans and Chinese, making deals in markets everywhere (Dotto 2019).

Africans in China profit from their work, but also contribute to the Chinese economy by selling and exporting Chinese products to Africa. The Guinean and Mali traders also bring goods from one country to sell in another country. However, they bring rough colored stones to be cut and treated in Chanthaburi. This way they add value to those raw materials and sell them for higher profit in the global market. They resemble the traders who send high-grade cocoa beans from Ghana and Côte d'Ivoire to be processed in Malaysia and Indonesia (Tan 2018).

The network of African gemstone traders in Chanthaburi is strong, but unlike the African community in Guangzhou (Li et al. 2009), it does not have the same connections to global networks nor is it well integrated within the Thai Gems Trading Association. The African gemstone traders in Chanthaburi have formed the African Gems Association in late 2019. The oversight committee is composed mainly of Guineans, with a small number of Mali, Ghanaian, and Senegalese traders. The main objective of the association is to strengthen the role of African traders in the local gems market, gain recognition, and connect to other networks.

The association has tried to form closer relationships with the Chanthaburi Gems and Jewelry Traders Association, but to no avail. The Secretary of the Chanthaburi Gems and Jewelry Traders Association told me: 'They keep asking [to join our group], but our committee has not accepted their request. Being a member of our association, would bring them recognition in the national and global gems market.' When asked for the reason of rejection, he answered:

> We do not reject their network, rather we consider them as individuals, we don't necessarily know much about their background. Moreover, our members have to pay a THB 2,000 annual membership. I am not sure their members would pay this amount. Besides, their association is very new, it was formed in late 2019.

It seems that the Secretary made a lot of assumptions about the African traders without checking them against reality. According to my interviews, staff members in African trading companies make approximately 20,000–30,000 THB/month; managers and company owners make considerably more. It seems that an annual membership fee of 2,000 THB would not pose an undue financial burden. Africans living in Chanthaburi contribute financially to other causes; most parents bring gifts for teachers and school staff on Children's Day or other occasions.

I posit that the Secretary of the Chanthaburi Gems and Jewelry Traders Association and its members use stereotypes about migrants being poor and unable to meet financial obligations to dismiss a more in-depth discussion of the association's decision to not accept African traders. I can only speculate that the reasons have more to do with Africans being othered by the association leaders and members than with their financial and economic standing.

### *Cultural integration*

Conventionally, cultural integration has been equated with immigrants' sense of belonging, measured by the quality of interaction between newcomers and members of the host society (Goździak 2005). Africans living in Chanthaburi have very limited social interactions with local Thais. Most African men usually stay in the gemstone market during weekends and in their offices during the week. If they go out for coffee, they frequent coffee shops in their neighborhood or in the vicinity of their trading companies and living areas. While there are no African-owned restaurants in

Chanthaburi, there are three halal restaurants and several street food vendors; a few of them are operated by African women catering to the local Muslim populations.

The African women living in Chanthaburi are very visible in public spaces. They frequent local markets to purchase foodstuffs. They take their children to school, but not knowing Thai they are unable to communicate with Thai parents or teachers. Language barrier seems to be the main factor impeding integration. Many also do not speak English, which might be helpful in communicating with some locals. A local merchant said:

> When they want to buy anything in the market, they point to what they want; they don't speak our language, only a few words. There are religious classes for African children and mothers sometime accompany their children, but usually stay in the corner listening to the teacher and don't associate with locals.

African immigrants interact with local residents most often at the mosque. The vast majority of Africans in Chanthaburi are Muslims. While Chanthaburi's residents are predominantly Buddhists (98%), followed by Christians (1.2%), there is a small Muslim minority (Ministry of Culture, Department of Religious Affairs 2017). There are a few prayer rooms set up in the business district and the local Thai Imam has also invited the African Imam and African community leaders to hold meetings and give talks to the African immigrants at the mosque. It seems that the African and local Muslims live side-by-side peacefully and support each other. When the Africans faced negative press in local social media, the Governor and other public authorities discussed this issue with the African community with support from the local imam. (MToday 2017). Africans have also been offered an ability to bury their dead, around 20 so far, in the mosque compound instead of sending the deceased back to Africa, which is costly. However, besides these few instances of cooperation, the province has not done anything to facilitate the African newcomers' integration.

### *Integration in schools*

The growth of the African population in Chanthaburi has resulted in an increased number of African children in the community. It is difficult to arrive at the exact number of African children living in Chanthaburi. In 2019, there were 43 African students in one of the local primary schools; mostly Guinean. They constitute approximately five percent of the total number of students in this school. Apart from the Guinean children, there is a small number of Cambodian and Vietnamese students in the same school.

The majority of the African children were born in Chanthaburi as children born in Africa do not follow their families to Thailand. A staff member in the public hospital made the following remark: 'We can always see pregnant African women around, some choose to go to a private hospital where they have less communication problem, but some choose to give birth in public hospitals; they know it costs less.' Pim, a 45-year-old Thai woman, added: 'They have many children. They are Muslim and don't use contraception. That will add up in the future.' These statements clearly indicate lack of acceptance of African children in the community and worry that the African community will get too large.

According to Thailand's education policy, non-Thai children are eligible to enroll in public schools. In accordance with the *Education for All* policy, the Thai government covers tuition fees, books, and uniforms for all children in K-12 education. In private schools, there are other costs that families have to pay out-of-pocket.

Many local schools have had non-Thai pupils in their classrooms, mainly from low-skilled Cambodian migrant workers' families. However, school administrators and teachers interviewed in the course of this study indicated that having African students in school is much more challenging than working with diverse Asian children as the cultural differences are greater. The teachers said that the most difficult time is during the first two years upon enrollment in school.

Most teachers have no formal preparation to teach foreign-born students and not all are willing to take on the task. Different schools use different approaches to solve this problem. One school has limited the number of African students so as to be able to cope with a diverse student body; another school has established a preparation class taught by a volunteer teacher. 'It's the teacher's duty, of course,' said one director, 'but many are not happy to teach African children. So, I asked for a volunteer teacher to start with kindergarten class and it came out very well.'

One of the volunteer teachers indicated that African students need more attention because of language barriers and cultural differences. The teacher has to be kind, patient, and work hard to facilitate students' adaptation to the new environment. One method that has worked well is a buddy system that pairs new African students with more experienced students who already speak Thai. The volunteer teacher I interviewed works both with African children and their guardians. 'I talk to students' parents coming to pick up their children or give a lift to children living in the same neighborhood. They are of the same ethnicity, they should help each other,' she said. The reason she volunteers is to ease the African children's transition into a Thai school, be more comfortable in a foreign country, and have less difficulty understanding people of different cultures. It is interesting that the buddy system does not involve native Thai students. Pairing Thai students with African pupils would go a long way towards enhancing cross-cultural understanding and breaking down the isolation of students from migrant families.

Some teachers said that African children are physically stronger and more aggressive than Thai students. 'They are strong and usually play with force. Other children are frightened and do not want to play with them, because they are afraid to be injured.' Thai girls avoid playing with African classmates, but boys play football together. African children are often bullied and discriminated against in schools. According to participants in a focus group, African students are not physically abused, but have to deal with racial slurs. Fatima, a 12-year-old Guinean girl said: 'I am called *edum* [impolite word for black girl] by my classmates, usually when we quarrel or compete in class. But I also heard a Thai boy being called an animal by an African girl.'

African children are not the only ones that are being bullied by Thai classmates. Cambodian and Vietnamese students face the same situation. They do not report bullying to the school administration, but they do fight back. When I asked a Thai schoolboy why he calls his African classmate *edum*, he answered that she has black skin; he claimed he did not mean to offend her. When I asked an African girl who was her best friend, she named a Thai girl, not an African classmate. All of the interviewed teachers were adamant that physical violence is not allowed in school, but many considered the 'verbal scolding' a normal practice among school children. Only one teacher indicated that she would try to stop verbal bullying.

It seems that dealing with bullying should not be left to the discretion of individual teachers who may or may not want to take on this task. Moreover, they may not be pedagogically prepared to counter school bullying. Provincial school authorities ought to tackle this problem, allocate resources, and provide training to school administrators and teachers.

In order to avoid racially based bullying, more affluent African parents send their children to international schools in Bangkok where racial bullying and discrimination is less common. Those who opt for public schools do so mainly for economic reasons as these schools are less expensive than private schools. Many African parents send their older children to be educated back in their countries of origin. There are various reasons for this practice. Some parents prefer their children to be educated in their native language or in English. One African father said: 'I prefer them to learn English or our language because it will be more beneficial than learning Thai.' Others think the youth will have fewer temptations back home. According to the African imam, parents believe that 'the atmosphere here is risky for their youths. In the home country, the youth can be controlled better.' Sending older children back to their countries of origin might indicate that the African families do not want to stay in Chanthaburi permanently and are not interested in long-term integration into the local community. On the other hand, it might be the best strategy available to them in the absence of provincial or national policies and programs tailored to foreign students. Generally speaking, African children that attend Thai public schools and learn Thai have a better chance of integrating into the local community than their parents who are reluctant to learn Thai and work and live isolated from the Thai community.

## Conclusions: fear of small numbers

For over two decades, African migrants lived peacefully alongside Thai residents in Chanthaburi. However, when the community reached some 700 members, complaints started surfacing on social media.

Why the negative reaction after two decades of peaceful coexistence? One reason articulated by many interviewees is the increasing number of Africans in the community. Compared with other immigrants in Chanthaburi, the number of Africans is very small. At 700 persons, Africans constitute only two percent of the 31,405 (as of December 2020) migrant workers working in the province (Chanthaburi Employment Office 2021).

African gemstone traders are considered skilled labor migrants. In contrast to low-skilled migrants working in agriculture and the service sector, skilled migrants are usually welcomed and appreciated by Thai hosts. However, some local residents believe that many Africans overstay their visas, work illegally, or are involved in criminal activities. A local resident remarked: 'We think some are staying illegally, do not have visa. There are many of them, that's why they make so much noise. They should learn how to live the way we live here.'

Indeed, several Thai residents complained that Africans disturb the serenity of the neighborhoods and cause tensions with local residents. Most Africans reside in five neighborhoods: two apartment complexes and three housing villages in Muang District, center of the province. Living together in large numbers encourages them to hang out at night, talk loudly outside, which causes negative reactions from locals. The complaints expressed by local Thais caught the attention of authorities. There are frequent immigration checks and scrutiny of supposedly illegal activities.

The African community leaders are aware of the locals' attitudes towards African traders and their families. They have attempted to reduce tensions and show concern. They have also made efforts to understand Thai culture. During the mourning period for the death of King Bhumibol (2016–17), the African community members showed their respect by marching from the mosque to the governor's office. Their expression of condolences relaxed the tensions and gained positive reaction from their neighbors.

Several of the local authority figures have rather positive views of the African residents in Chanthaburi. They do not perceive them as problematic. 'Compared to Africans elsewhere, here they don't create any problems, no drugs or criminal cases,' indicated one of the interviewed immigration officers. The assessment of the Africans in Chanthaburi is similar to the perceptions of Africans in Yiwu village, Zhejiang, China, where they live more harmoniously with local Chinese than those in Guangzhou that were not treated well and faced more discrimination (Bodomo & Ma 2010).

Local Thai residents, perhaps influenced by accounts in mass media, fear illegal activities: immigration violations, drug trafficking, and other forms of crime. These misperceptions might be a function of cultural differences and lack of meaningful relationships between African and Thai residents.

The police tried to narrow the cultural gap by organizing a cultural training for African migrants. Interestingly, they have not thought about training programs for the police force to understand the cultures of their African neighbors. African community and Thai community leaders signed a Memorandum of Understanding (MOU) to promote better understanding between Africans and local residents (Chanthaburi Cultural Office 2019). 'So far, they seem to cooperate with authorities in any way they can, apart from a few who overstay their visa, they haven't been charged with any criminal cases,' remarked one of the Thai officials.

As already mentioned, Chanthaburi is not a monocultural province. Historically, it has been a melting pot of Chinese, Indian, Cambodian, Laotian, and Burmese migrants. While these groups are culturally diverse, they have integrated into the local community well; there has never been any serious conflict or violence between and among the migrant communities and the host society. I posit that while Asian migrants are ethnically diverse, they are culturally similar to Thais. There is also a pan-Asian affinity with members of other ASEAN countries. Africans are racially, ethnically, and culturally distant. The African community is small but their 'loud and noisy' voices do not fit the local cultural norms. The language barrier does not facilitate communication, social interactions, and integration. Most Africans have very little facility in Thai compared to unskilled Cambodian, Burmese, or Vietnamese working in Chanthaburi.

It seems that the African community in Chanthaburi is an example of segmented assimilation, a theory that suggests different immigrant groups assimilate into different segments of society (Zhou 1997; Portes et al. 2005). They are certainly gainfully (self)employed and able to support their families albeit not always accepted by the Thai trading associations. They play an important role in the gems trading industry, but their businesses benefit only a small group of elite traders, not the wider community. The wider Thai society is of the opinion that African gemstone traders do not contribute to the local economy as they do not create jobs, they mainly hire other Africans. In contrast, Chinese migrants from mainland China set up companies to export local fruits to China (Kamonpetch & Jitpong 2021). They act as brokers who create more value for local fruit produce. The African migrants in Chanthaburi do not purchase any local products for export. They are entrenched in the niche economy as gemstone traders, while local artisans cut the gems and make jewelry.

It remains to be seen whether the African community will become a bridge for Africa–Thailand relations the way the African community in Guangzhou has served in this role (Bodomo 2010). At present, the Africans in Chanthaburi are isolated from the Thai community and live in an ethnic ghetto. Following Bodomo's assertions, I suggest that both the Thai and the various African governments should work towards eliminating the animosities towards African gems traders and harness the contributions of the African community to promote socio-economic relations between Africa and Thailand.

## References

Appadurai, Arjun. (2006). *Fear of Small Numbers: An Essay on the Geography of Anger*. Durham, NC: Duke University Press.

Berry, Sara. (2004). 'Value and Ambiguity: Evidence and Ideas from African Niche Economies,' *African Economic History* 32, pp. 143–151.

Bhattacharya, Sreedeep, Chowdhury, Arnab Roy, & Abid, Ahmed. (2017). 'A Market Like You've Never Seen,' *The Hindu*, 29 July. Available at: https://www.thehindu.com/thread/arts-culture-society/a-market-like-youve-never-sheen/article19384978.ece.

Bodomo, Adams. (2010). 'The African Trading Community in Guangzhou: An Emerging Bridge for Africa–China Relations,' *The China Quarterly* 203, pp. 693–707.

Bodomo, Adams & Ma, Grace. (2010). 'From Guangzhou to Yiwu: Emerging Facets of the African Diaspora in China,' *International Journal of African Renaissance Studies – Multi-, Inter- and Transdisciplinarity* 5(2), pp. 283–289.

Bonacich, Edna. (1973). 'A Theory of Middleman Minorities,' *American Sociological Review* 38(5), pp. 583–594.

Chantavanich, Supang & Triemwittaya, Chada. (2020). *Chinese Community in Bangkok and Migration Phenomena*. Bangkok: Institute of Asian Studies.

Chanthaburi Employment Office. (2021). 'Statistic of Registered Migrant Workers,' Available at: https://www.doe.go.th/prd/chanthaburi/service/param/site 99/cat/17/sub/0/pull/detail/view/detail/object_id/839.

Chetpatanawanich, Kriengsak & Reungviset, Pariachart. (1995). 'Chanthaburi, City of Earth Resource,' In: *Sarakadee: Chanthaburi*, edited by Parichart Reungviset, pp. 22–49. Bangkok: Sarakadee Press.

Dotto, C. (2019). 'Little Africa in China,' *New Internationalist*, October 30. Available at: https://newint.org/features/2019/03/11/%E2%80%98little-africa %E2%80%99-china.

Duggleby, Luke. (2014). 'Tricks and Stones: The Gem Traders of Chanthaburi,' *Post Magazine*, 9 August. Available at: https://www.scmp.com/magazines/post -magazine/article/1569045/tricks-and-stones.

GIA. (2015). 'Venture into Chanthaburi's Sapphire Mines and Markets with GIA's Field Gemologists,' *GIA*, 23 October. Available at: https://www.gia.edu/gia -news-research/chanthaburi-sapphire-mines-markets-field-gemology.

Goździak, Elzbieta M. (2005). 'New Immigrant Communities and Integration,' In: *Beyond the Gateway: Immigrants in a Changing America*, edited by Elzbieta M. Goździak and Susan F. Martin, pp. 3–17. Lanham, MD: Lexington Books.

Guyer, Jane. (1997). *An African Niche Economy: Farming to Feed Ibadan 1968– 1988*. Edinburgh: Edinburgh University Press.

Hughes, Richard. (2010). 'History of Chanthaburi and Pailin: Moontown,' *Lotus Gemology*, 1 June. Available at: https://www.ruby-sapphire.com/articles/876 -history-of-chanthaburi-pailin-moontown.

Harkins, B. (2019). *Thailand Migration Report 2019*. Bangkok: International Organization for Migration. Available at: https://thailand.iom.int/sites/ thailand/files/document/publications/Thailand%20Report%202019_22012019 _LowRes.pdf.

Hayami, Yoko. (2006). 'Redefining "Otherness" from Northern Thailand Introduction: Notes Towards Debating Multiculturalism in Thailand and Beyond,' *Southeast Asian Studies* 44(3), pp. 283–294.

Huguet, Jerrold, Chamratrithirong, Aphichat, & Natali, Claudia. (2012). 'Thailand at a Crossroads: Challenges and Opportunities in Leveraging Migration for Development,' *Issue in Brief 6*. Available at: https://www.migrationpolicy.org/ pubs/LeveragingMigration.pdf.

Hunter, Marcena & Lawson, Lynda. (2020). 'A Rough-Cut Trade: Africa's Colored Gemstone Flows to Asia,' Available at: https://globalinitiative.net/analysis/africa -asia-gemstones-trade/.

Kmonpetch, Aungkhana & Jitpong, Waranya. (2021). 'Thai Exports of Longan to China: Implications of Chinese Investment on Thai Stakeholders,' In: *Global Production Networks a Rural Development: Southeast Asia as a Fruit Supplier to China*, edited by Bill Pritchard. Elgaronline. Available at: https://elgaronline .com/view/edcoll/9781800883871/9781800883871.xml.

Li, Zhigang, Ma, Lawrence, J. C., & Desheng, Xue. (2009). 'An African enclave in China: The making of a new transnational urban space,' *Eurasian Geography and Economics* 50(6), pp. 699–719.

Ministry of Culture, Department of Religious Affairs. (2017). 'Chanthabun Riverside Community, Multicultural Society, Way of Chanthabun People,' *Religion Direct Line* 15(1), p. 12.

MToday. (2017). *Thais Are Frightened of Lots of Africans in Chanthaburi, the Governor Rushes to Discuss the Problem but the News is Taken to Distort and Slander Muslim MToday*, 30 June. Available at: https://www.mtoday.co.th/11598.

OECD/ILO. (2017). *How Immigrants Contribute to Thailand's Economy*. Paris: OECD Publishing. Available at: https://www.ilo.org/global/topics/labour -migration/publications/WCMS_613491.

Office of Provincial Commercial Affairs Chanthaburi. (2021). *Data of Registered Trading Companies in Chanthaburi*.

Pardieu, Vincent. (2019). *Thailand: The Undisputed Ruby Trading Kingdom, A Brief History*. Available at: https://www.researchgate.net/publication/339439253 _Thailand_the_undisputed_ruby_trading_kingdom_a_brief_history.

Pawlak, Marek & Goździak, Elzbieta M. (2019). 'Multiple Belongings: Transnational Mobility, Social Class, and Gendered Identities Among Polish Migrants in Norway,' *Social Identities* 26(1), pp. 77–91. https://doi.org/10.1080 /13504630.2019.1677458.

Portes, Alejandro. (1994). 'The Informal Economy and Its Paradoxes,' In: *The Handbook of Economic Sociology*, edited by Neil J. Smelser & Richard Swedberg, pp. 426–449. Princeton, NJ: Princeton University Press.

Portes, Alejandro, Fernandez-Kelly, Patricia, & Haller, William. (2005). 'Segmented Assimilation on the Ground: The New Second Generation in Early Adulthood,' *Ethnic and Racial Studies* 28(6), pp. 1000–1040.

Ray, Brian. (2002). 'Immigrant Integration: Building to Opportunity,' *Migration Information Source*. Available at: https://www.migrationpolicy.org/article/ immigrant-integration-building-opportunity.

Schrover, Marlou. (2001). 'Immigrant Business and Niche Formation in Historical Perspective: The Netherlands in the Nineteenth Century,' *Journal of Ethnic and Migration Studies* 27(2), pp. 295–311.

Smyth, H. Warrington. (1898). *Five Years in Siam, from 1891 to 1996*. Reprint 1994. Bangkok: White Lotus Press.

Tan, Kelvin. (2018). 'Africa-Asia Trade Finance Gap: Time to Take Stock,' *African Business Magazine*, 14 August. Available at: https://african.business/2018/08/ economy /africa-asia-trade-finance-gap-time-to-take-stock/.

Waldinger, Roger. (1996). *Still the Promised City? African-Americans and New Immigrants in Postindustrial New York*. Cambridge, MA: Harvard University Press.

Zhou, Min. (1997). 'Segmented Assimilation: Issues, Controversies and Recent Research on the New Second Generation,' *International Migration Review* 31(4), pp. 975–1008.

# 8 Following the ball

## Thailand, the new frontier for African footballers

*Gabriela Romero and*
*Nithis Thammasaengadipha*

## Introduction

Migration of footballers is often linked to globalization, a process fueled by and resulting in increased cross-border flows of goods, services, money, people, information, and culture (Lago-Peñas et al. 2019). However, some scholars contest this assertion. Matthew Taylor (2006) sees a significant flaw in much of the literature on sports and globalization. He argues that such conceptualization stems from insensitivity to historical change. 'If football is the global sport *par excellence*,' he writes, 'it arguably became so as early as 1930, when 13 national teams headed to Uruguay to compete in the first World Cup competition' (Taylor 2006: 8). Taylor posits that the establishment of the World Cup expanded the international market for football players from the beginning. Furthermore, Taylor suggests that 'international migration of football players should be seen as one of ebb and flow rather than a straightforward increase and growth.' Taylor also indicates that mobility of footballers 'has been affected by economic and political processes and by the restrictions of states and governments, as well as regulations of national and international football federations' (Taylor 2006: 13).

Mass media introduced football to the wider Thai society in the late 1960s. In 1966, Thai television stations broadcast the final FIFA World Cup match between England and West Germany to the applause of many Thai fans. In 1970, the Thai television broadcast the World Cup live for the first time. From then on, televised European football matches became very popular among Thai football enthusiasts. By the 1990s, football became both an entertainment and a leisure activity for the Thai middle class. But it was not until the late 1990s that Thailand established professional football leagues.

Since 2007, the Thai League has gone from strength to strength and has seen the rise of several clubs. FIFA's decision to expand the World Cup bodes well for Thailand (Murphy 2017). Football's increasing popularity in Thailand created a socio-cultural space where players and spectators from

DOI: 10.4324/9781003286554-8

diverse countries and cultural backgrounds interact and build new realities. African football players have been crucial to the rising profile of the Thai Professional League (TPL). Almost every TPL team has at least one African player and some have as many as half a dozen players that add foreign experience, tactical adaptability, and physicality to the team's options. Despite a recent rule change that allows only three foreign players plus one extra foreign player from within Asia on the pitch at the same time, Africans continue to play for Thai clubs (Erker 2012) although some teams are replacing African players with European footballers (Murphy 2016).

Although football is very popular in Thailand, there is limited scholarship on African footballers in Thailand – nothing compared to the magnitude of scholarly publications on African footballers in Europe (e.g., Cleveland 2017; Akindes 2013; Poli 2010). Most publications are interviews or media articles. However, there are emerging scholars who write about football in Thailand. Some of these writings are not necessarily about African players, but more broadly about the evolution of the game in Thailand (e.g., Panarut 2014; Kookannog 2006). Articles on mobility of African footballers occasionally mention players working in Thailand (e.g., Ungruhe & Esson 2017). Akindes (2013) discusses the emerging Asian trajectories of the African players' migrations and examines the particularities and the impact that Asian migration has had on the emergence of the semi-peripheral football economy located in South and Southeast Asia.

Many African players arrive in Thailand when in their teens and in a sense grow up in the country. A number of footballers stay in Thailand following their retirement. Who are they? Why do they come to Thailand? How well are they adapting to local life and football tactics? Given Thais' unfamiliarity with Africans and prejudices against Black people, do they experience discrimination? We attempt to answer some of these questions in this chapter. We showcase several Africans who migrated to Thailand to be part of professional football clubs. The narratives we elicited from them offer an insight into their motivation to come to Thailand and into their integration both on and off the football field.

We begin with remarks on the theoretical framework that best suits our analysis of African footballers' integration into the Thai football teams and the broader Thai society. The crux of the article is an analysis of narratives elicited from selected football players and coaches to explore factors that have influenced their mobility and brought them to Thailand. We also examine the strategies and resources that our interlocutors mobilized in their effort to integrate into the Thai football leagues and maintain connections with families in countries of origin. We situate this analysis within the South–South migration framework, away from colonial and postcolonial perspectives customarily used for the exploration of the cultural and economic dimensions of the labor migration of African footballers to Europe.

## Theorizing migration and football

Migration of professional footballers has received a lot of attention in migration studies. Scholars use a wide range of theoretical frameworks within which to analyze mobility of African footballers. James Esson (2015, 2013) underscores the fact that research on football migration has recently undergone a significant transformation.

Since the vast majority of research on African footballers focuses on migration of African players to Europe, initially many scholars deployed a colonial and neocolonial perspective in their studies (Darby et al. 2007; Bale & Maguire 1994; Magee & Sugden 2002) and relied on a South–North migration movement for their analysis (Nawyn 2016). They saw mobility of African footballers to Europe as symptomatic of relations between the core (Europe) and the periphery (Africa), and the domination of the former over the latter (Darby 2011). Others wrote about circuits of power (Cornelissen & Solberg 2007). Carter (2013) and Darby (2013) theorized migration of African footballers using actor network theory and global value chains, respectively.

It is beyond the scope of this chapter to review all theories used to debate migration of footballers. In this exploratory study, we were not concerned with macro analyses, but rather with the *emic* (or insiders') perspectives of what it means to be an African footballer in Thailand. We have been particularly drawn to Ungruhe and Esson's study of Ghanaian footballers in which they examine the perceptions and hopes of young West Africans who believe that 'migration through football provides a way to achieve social standing and improve one's life chances' (2017: 23). They focus on the social dimension of hope (Hage 2003) and argue that the hope of social becoming is a collective practice to overcome one's state of what Bloch (1986) calls the state of *not-yet*. They emphasize the importance *of becoming a somebody* to the generation of young men. They also observe that economic uncertainty, political unrest, and the reconfiguration of established cultural practices obstruct social mobility and trajectories to *become somebody*.

## The arrival of African players in Thailand

The history of African football dates back to the colonial times, but it is its post-colonial evolution that led to the emergence of players distinguished by game intelligence, technical finesse, and playful flair. Currently, Africa is the third-largest exporter of footballers in the world (Akindes 2013). African football players' skills combined with FIFA's efforts to recognize football teams outside Europe contributed to the recognition of African players in Asia. By the mid-1990s, several dozen African players joined football teams in Thailand, Singapore, Indonesia, and Cambodia (Cho 2016; Erker 2012).

Undoubtedly, Europe remains the preferred destination for African footballers because that is where they can *become someone*, achieve celebrity status, and earn good money. However, a path to a European league is very competitive. Many African players prefer to build their careers in Asia. Asian countries also hold an economic advantage over the Sub-Saharan region. Simultaneously, many Asian leagues look up to the athleticism of African players (Akindes 2013). As Abe (2018) writes, African players scale up the Southeast Asian football scene. They are hardworking. They exhibit distinct play styles, winning tactics, and physical prowess. This unique form of social capital serves them well in Thailand.

Reminiscing about foreign football players in Thailand, the chairman of the Thailand Online Sports Correspondents Association recalled seeing Africans playing football for leisure at the Royal Plaza (*Sanam Luang*) some 30 years ago. According to Mr. Khwankaew, the best-known African player at that time was Billy Yeab, who played forward for Thailand Tobacco Monopoly Football Club. At first, most of the African footballers came to Thailand on a tourist visa and negotiated with football clubs to participate in the tryouts without the help of an agent. They lived and worked in Khao San Road and Pratu Nam and spent their free time playing football and walking from club to club for tryouts. They did not have much social standing either back home or in Thailand, but they had a desire to become somebody and worked hard to achieve this status.

Adebayo Gbadebo, a footballer from Nigeria, was the first African player recruited by a Thai football club, the Police Tero Football Club in Bangkok. Gbadebo helped the team win the 2000/2001 Thai Premier League Championship. Starting in 2007, Gbadebo began his coaching career. In 2010, he became the assistant coach in the Thai Professional League. Currently, he is the head coach of Suphanburi FC.

Africans played a significant role in the Thai Premier League Company Limited since its establishment in 2009. After Dagno Siaka from the Ivory Coast joined Muangthong United, the team won three championships between 2009 and 2012. Robert Procureur, a Belgian team manager with connections to football academies in Africa, recruited several Africans to play in Thailand, among them such high-profile players as Dagno Siaka and Soumahoro Yaya. The players were attracted by the growth of the Thai League and resulting earnings (Sports 442 Editor, Interview, May 23, 2018).

Thai clubs sought African players because of their physical and mental attributes: height, strength, and endurance. Africans were particularly suitable as midfielders. Midfielders are generally positioned on the field between their team's defenders and forwards. Most managers assign at least one midfielder to disrupt the opposing team's attacks, while others may be tasked with creating goals, or have equal responsibilities between attack and defense. Midfielders are the players who typically travel the greatest distance during a match. Midfielders arguably have the most possession during a game, and thus they are among the fittest players on the pitch.

Africans are also attractive to Thai clubs, because they command lower salaries than footballers from South America and Western Europe. In 2021, the top player from Brazil earned 1.5 million baht/month, whereas the top African players earned between 200,000 and 500,000 baht/month. This is advantageous to football clubs. Coaches and club managers prize African players' adaptability and fighting spirit. Many players know basic football terminology in Thai. Some speak Thai because they have Thai wives.

Despite a large number of Thai agencies recruiting foreign players, most African footballers are walk-ins asking to participate in tryouts with teams in Thai League 3 and Amateur League. These Africans often lead precarious lives as they travel from club to club in search of a team. Those who do get hired command comparatively low salaries (anywhere from 20,000 to 30,000 baht/month) when compared with African footballers in prestigious clubs. Given the low cost of living in Bangkok, these salaries seem adequate.

The demands for African players in the Thai League 1 have declined since 2012 as the growing league started searching for more marketable players. Muangthong United replaced their African players with Europeans. Buriram United hired Spanish and Latin American players and later won five championships. As a result, many teams in the Thai Premier League became interested in recruiting European and Latin American players. Starting in 2015, Latin American players far outnumbered African footballers.

Figure 8.1 presents the origins of foreign players in the Thai League 1.

In 2015, the Thai Premier League changed the rules regarding the number of foreign players on Thai teams. Previously, each team could hire as many as seven foreign players. Currently, only five foreign players are allowed; at least one of the five foreign players must be Asian. Under this condition, the top teams prefer higher quality players from Europe and South America, especially Brazil. Despite preferences for South American players, several Africans still play in the Thai Premier League. Additionally, many lower-ranked teams prefer African players, because of their adaptability, resilience, and playing style that suit the counter-attack tactics often used in the games (Manager of Chamchuri United, Interview, May 25, 2018).

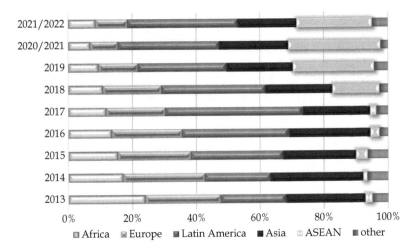

*Figure 8.1* Origins of foreign players in each Thai Premier League season. Source: Transfermarkt, n.d., Thai League - Players from foreign clubs, retrieved from https://www.transfermarkt.com/thai-league/gastarbeiter/wettbewerb/THA1/saison_id

## Findings and analysis

Lured by the media coverage of professional football and the seemingly glamorous lives of star footballers, many young Africans see football as a means of upward economic and social mobility (Christensen & Sørensen 2009; Poli 2010) and as a way to *become somebody* (Ungruhe & Esson 2017).

Attractive salaries are definitely a pull factor attracting young African footballers to Southeast Asia. Pay differential, however, is not the only reason for seeking better circumstances in Thailand. Steve, a football coach, talked about the challenges African players face in their home countries to enter a good football league. 'Competition is stiff and expectations are great,' said Steve. Physical demands and psychological pressure stemming from the need to play against younger and physically stronger footballers create a fierce competition and push many African players into markets where the supply of players is lower. Comparing his experience in Thailand with the situation in Angola, Arnoldo explained how football in Thailand is different: 'Thai football is faster and it requires less physical effort. In Angola, both the training and the matches were more physically demanding. It was all about endurance and physical performance.'

While some African footballers succeed and meet their aspirations, many do not recognize the precarious nature of a career in professional football, but nevertheless want to pursue their dreams (Esson 2013). Research has shown that the pursuit of football stardom often comes at the expense of formal education (see Bourke 2003; Darby 2010; Donnelly & Petherick 2004), leaving these men with few options when their careers end or never take off. While playing football in Mozambique, Arnoldo enrolled in a business administration program at a local university. His father demanded he pursue higher education as a condition to allow Arnoldo to play football. However, once he became a sought-after footballer, Arnoldo abandoned his studies.

## Seeking greener pastures in Thailand

Many young Africans see the path to football stardom as a means to escape poverty and an avenue for upward mobility. Akindes (2013) reported that in 2007, in African leagues, the average pay was $2,800. Furthermore, in most Sub-Saharan professional leagues a steady income for players is not the norm. Darby (2008) noted that the average salary in the Ghanaian premier league was $100 to $300/month.

While salaries in Asia might be better than in Africa, there is still a significant salary disparity between different Asian countries: foreign players can earn up to $2,000/month in Bangladesh or $9,000 in Thailand; top players in Indonesia earn around $80,000/year, with star players in Vietnam earning $200,000–$300,000/year (Luedi 2018). Recruiters use these exponentially higher salaries to entice young footballers to make the journey to Asia.

In media interviews, African players report that they make two to three times as much in Thailand as they did back home. One player indicated that his starting salary amounted to $9,200 (Siriwat & Brill 2015), a sum he would never have been able to command at home. A possibility of better earnings motivated several of our interlocutors. Arnoldo was born in Angola, but when he was four years old, his family moved to Portugal. Seeing his older brother, Ryan, play football for many years, Arnoldo fell in love with the sport. He enrolled in the *Football Academy of Coimbra* to become a professional player. After many years of preparation and training, Arnoldo achieved his dream. Over the next several years, he played in nine clubs in five countries, including his native Angola, his adopted homeland of Portugal, as well as Qatar, Tunisia, and finally Thailand.

'The curiosity for other cultures and new challenges motivated me to move to Thailand,' said Arnoldo. 'Of course, the economic benefits were also important.' The pasture was definitely greener in Thailand. As a professional player, Arnoldo enjoyed a better quality of life than the one he had in Angola or even in Portugal. He liked the low cost of living in Thailand and access to healthcare services paid for by his club.

Arnoldo enjoyed his experience playing for a Thai team. However, after his contract ended, Arnoldo went back to Europe to join a 'higher quality of football and find more opportunities' as well as higher pay. He does not exclude the possibility of returning to Thailand. However, since he has Portuguese citizenship, he plans to retire in Portugal and become a wellness coach. 'I also have a dream of attending a nutrition school and helping people to achieve a healthier life,' he told me. Being a professional football player with years of international experience, Arnoldo does well wherever he goes. It seems that he has become *somebody*, a coveted player that finds a spot for himself on different teams in different countries. He might be able to attract other athletes to work with him on their wellness once he gets appropriate credentials.

Mamadou, a player from Cameroon, said: 'At the beginning I was scared to ask for much money. They paid me 8,000 THB/month plus rent.' Mamadou admitted that he did not know much about contract negotiations. Initially, he was less interested in the conditions of his employment and more in the opportunity to immerse himself in the Thai football. However, with experience came more money and better deals. Mamadou played with ten different teams. By the time he turned 23, Mamadou became very popular with Thai football teams, and they sought him out. 'I had many offers,' he said. 'I decided to play with Ratchaburi. I earned 100,000 THB/month and 500 THB/month for training. I played with them for one year.'

In one interview, Mamadou remembered how happy he was to be able to prove that he was a player worth good money. He also became bolder and went searching for better deals. He recalled a situation when he just went up to a coach and introduced himself. The coach looked at Mamadou with curiosity and invited him to join the practice. 'The same day,' recalls Mamadou, 'I signed a contract.' Mamadou kept on changing teams to get a better deal and to improve his game.

During his years as a professional player in Thailand, Mamadou got offers from teams in Malaysia, but he didn't want to leave Thailand. 'I didn't want to start my life again; by that time Thailand was my home,' he said. He described his experience in Thailand as an opportunity that allowed him to support his family and achieve his dreams: 'With this job I am able to help my mum and my family back home; I built a home for my father and paid for the schooling of my brothers.' Oko, another Cameroonian, compared favorably the salary and living conditions in Thailand. 'Sometimes in Cameroon they never pay me, or they take months to pay me for my job,' he said.

### *Thai football leagues recruiting football players*

There are considerable differences in the recruitment processes and paths for African football players heading to Asia, compared to those going to

Europe. Well-established European professional football clubs utilize academies with joint-ventures in Africa and they constantly scout African competitions. In Europe, football players work with agents and coaches when they want to switch teams or get a better contract (De Latour 2010). Thai leagues don't have football academies and do not hold competitions.

Recruitment of African footballers to Asia displays many similarities with the irregular migration of African players to Europe. Many young African footballers enter Asian countries on tourist visas hoping to land positions with local clubs. Arriving as tourists, many footballers linger waiting for an offer, which results in their visas expiring. Stuck in Thailand with no money and no immigration status, some African footballers face poverty, but even those who manage to get a position with a club find themselves at the mercy of their employers. With no valid visa, players are also at a loss to report any abuse for fear of being deported.

Arnoldo was one of the lucky ones. In the fall of 2017, Ubon United Football Club approached Arnoldo to play for them. The club took care of Arnoldo's visa and work permit. Arnoldo is a naturalized citizen of Portugal and said that his Portuguese nationality certainly helped facilitate the immigration process. Finding suitable accommodations was one of his biggest challenges. 'Most of the football teams take the responsibility of finding housing for their players,' he said, 'but in my case it was different.' He explained that in the future he would like to have financial and logistical support from the club. Despite less than optimal conditions, Arnoldo played with Ubon United for 11 months.

Many African players are recruited on the recommendation of another player (Akindes 2013). Most of our interlocutors came to Thailand on the recommendation of friends that were already playing for Thai leagues. When asked how he ended up playing for a Thai team, Arnoldo said: 'It was not an agent. A friend of mine was playing in Thailand and he introduced me to his team. I hoped they would recruit me.' After being introduced to the team, Arnoldo was asked to come to the next training and observe to learn more about the team's tactics and strategies. A week later, after getting comfortable with the team members, Arnoldo was able to join the training and eventually joined the second part of the season.

Mamadou, originally from Cameroon, has been playing football in Thailand for the past 12 years. He contacted a friend who was playing football in Thailand to learn about opportunities. In 2006, Mamadou traveled to Thailand on a tourist visa. Once he signed his first contract, the team helped Mamadou to get a work permit and extend his visa for two years. 'I just had to sign the papers and sometimes go to the immigration office.' He never had trouble renewing his visa; every time he changed teams, they took care of extending his visa and his work permit. When we last spoke, Mamadou had a non-immigrant business visa and a work permit that allowed him to keep playing in the Thai League.

It seems that Mamadou was one of the lucky ones. Lack of regulations and structured recruitment processes leave space for exploitation. Jeremy Luedi (2018) reported a high-profile case from Laos. In early 2015, the global players union FIFPro investigated the illegal transfer of 23 African footballers as young as 14 to an unregistered football academy in Laos, by the Laotian team, Champasak United. The players were forced to sign six-year contracts. Despite being promised $200/month and accommodation, the players were never paid and were confined to the club's stadium.

### *Falling prey to unscrupulous scouts*

A growing number of Africans are looking for professional football opportunities in Asia. However, a far smaller number of available positions has led to the emergence of unscrupulous agents who take advantage of the dreams of young Africans (Luedi 2018).

In 2011, *The Daily Guide Accra* reported that 70 Ghanaian youth were tricked into thinking that they were being recruited for football trials in Mauritius. Individuals claiming to be football scouts approached the young men and pledged to make appropriate arrangements in exchange for several thousand Ghanaian Cedis to cover the players' travel costs and agents' commissions (Coe & Wiser 2011, cited in Esson 2015). A Cameroonian agent, speaking about the situation in Thailand, described how 'out of forty players officially under contract and playing for a team there are fifty others in the street without contracts or means of living' (Luedi 2018).

Having played football in Thailand for many years, Mamadou recognizes the hardships some African footballers face. He witnessed young men becoming victims of scams by fake agents, promising them to find outstanding opportunities. Mamadou tried to help some young Africans realize what they have to offer, but he also explained how these young players sometimes become victims of exploitation.

When he first arrived in Thailand in 2006, Oko intended to become a professional football player, but he soon realized that he might try to become a football agent. He realized that there were many young African boys who came to Thailand to become professional players, but most of them were being exploited: 'Many of them used to work without a salary or sometimes just for $50/month, sleeping on the floor. … Everybody in Africa thinks that football is an easy way to have a good life until they face reality.' Oko decided to help these young African boys. He got together with his Thai friend and they created a group of young players from different African countries to play together and to bring them in to the first or second divisions to improve their skills. 'We started with a group of 30 players between 16 and 25 years old,' reminisced Oko. Kwame, Oko's friend facilitated contact with football clubs and secured invitations to bring the young players to friendly matches so they could show their skills. The beginning was challenging, but after a couple of months, Oko managed to secure a few deals with Thai teams for his players and his name became known in the Thai football world.

Oko says he feels responsible for the football players and their living conditions. He tries to make sure that both the teams and the players fulfill their promises. 'Of course, I also have many cases where players break the contracts. For young guys, it could sometimes be hard to deal with fame and money.' He seems to think that Asia is not for very young players. He advises them to start their football careers in Europe. This advice contradicts what we have heard from other interlocutors; most people felt that starting in Asia provides African footballers with a springboard and gives them an opportunity to hone their skills before they set their sights on Europe. We heard from some of the interviewed footballers that they came to Asia, because it is 'an easy option; players don't need to be too good to be able to play professionally.' Also, players who might be considered too old to play in Europe, get a chance in Thailand.

These stories indicate that the path to *become somebody* is not easy. Young Africans who speak English or Thai might have other opportunities, but without much formal education and language capability, they either have to go back to Africa or lead precarious lives in Thailand.

### *Becoming part of the team and integration into the wider Thai society*

African footballers playing in Thailand have different opinions about integration challenges. Obinna Nnodim, a Nigerian player who goes locally by the name Emmanuel, said: 'There is glamour in the Thai game now and a good atmosphere.' Emmanuel played in his native Nigeria, and in Malaysia, Oman, and Vietnam before coming to Bangkok to have a reconstructive surgery on his knee. He seems to have adjusted well to working and living in Thailand.

'Adjusting to the Thai game is also not so difficult,' he said. 'Communication is important, but it's the same thing in Germany or any other foreign league' (Erker 2012). Emmanuel's opinion is not necessarily shared by others. Neither Armando nor Mamadou spoke any Thai when they arrived in Bangkok and found the language barrier a challenge to integration into the Thai League and the broader society. Arnoldo and two Brazilian players had a Portuguese translator to help them during training and matches. Mamadou admitted that the beginnings were not easy. It took him some time to get used both to the Thai lifestyle and to the Thai football dynamics. During the first four years, Mamadou did not go to Cameroon. He focused solely on his football career. His friend, Abyoye, introduced him to his team. Mamadou participated in one training session and afterwards the coach invited Mamadou to join the team. Once he joined the team, he made a decision to learn Thai. Today, his fluency in Thai gives him more opportunities to join Thai teams coached by Thai coaches and allows him to participate in Thai social events, watch Thai TV, and speak with his Thai neighbors.

Being well connected to his Thai team members and neighbors doesn't mean he lost contact with other Africans. He likes to be surrounded by friends who share the same culture and language. However, he explained that he never felt like an outsider playing on Thai teams. 'We didn't have any problems because football is the same everywhere,' he said. 'When we meet in the field everyone knows what to do.' The only time he felt excluded was when he played on a Thai team coached by a Brazilian coach. The coach expelled Mamadou, because 'he couldn't communicate' with him. Mamadou thinks it was not an issue of language *per se* but rather a clash of personalities.

Like Mamadou, Oko invested time and energy into learning Thai. He attributes his success to his fluency in Thai. 'It was necessary for my work,' he said. As an agent, Oko gets a cut of 10 to 15 percent from each contract he secures for his clients. Oko has recently branched out to other countries trying to recruit more football players and working in partnership with agents in Europe. Oko also observed that recently Thai society has become more open-minded, more understanding, and accepting of foreigners, which helps in making new friends.

As much as Oko enjoys working in Thailand, he sees the effects of new migration laws on the players. For example, the new law stipulates that players must extend their visas in their home countries. It is inconvenient and costly. 'Before it was easier, they could go to Laos and Cambodia to extend but nowadays they have to go back to Africa.' According to Oko, the new laws foster criminality. African players and their families send money to fake football agents in Thailand in order to get assistance with visa renewals and end up being cheated.

Arnoldo said that even though he didn't speak Thai, after a while, the Thai culture 'was an easy culture to adapt. Arnoldo admired Thai players' ability to be present in the moment. In his opinion, their mindfulness allows them to not think about previous mistakes. As a result, they are in a better position to make decisions on the field. Emmanuel also said that cultural adjustments are not as big an obstacle as the bureaucratic problems if a player doesn't have a team lined up.

# Conclusions

Our research suggests that migration of African footballers to Thailand does not always begin with the demand for African talent or recruitment by unscrupulous agents (see Esson 2015 for comparison of findings). Rather, prompted by poverty or lack of opportunities in their origin countries, young Africans seek opportunities abroad hoping that their young and healthy bodies as well as their love of football will aid them in *becoming somebody*. Ungruhe and Esson (2017: 37) posit that these young men migrate not because they are footballers. 'Rather, the attraction of a career in football is the outcome of broader structural changes taking place within [...] society, which, in the absence of state welfare provision, encourages young people to be job creators, not job seekers.'

While footballers such as Arnoldo trained with football academies to become professional players, many other players we met played football recreationally and traveled to Thailand to seek better livelihoods. They thought they would be able to support themselves and send remittances to their families by playing football. Indeed, several of the interviewed Africans managed to build decent livelihoods in Thailand and support their families at home. Oko, who initially wanted to become a footballer, soon realized that he might be better off working as an agent. His intuition was correct. With his earnings, Oko supported his mother in Cameroon, built a house for his father, and paid his brothers' school fees.

We met other aspiring footballers who were not able to realize their dreams. Those lacking educational capital and ability to speak Thai were in a particularly precarious situation. However, those who learned Thai and had educational credentials managed to build professional careers. One of our interlocutors spoke very good English and ended up teaching English in elementary school. He and his family seem to be very well-integrated in Thailand.

Like most other sports, football is not a sport that can be played into old age. Therefore, the question remains: What will happen to those players who no longer can play football? Will they stay in Thailand or go back to Africa? While most of our interlocutors achieved the status of a good football player, will this short-term accomplishment translate into a long-term good socio-economic standing? With a couple of exceptions, most of the interviewed players do not have other qualifications that would enable them to thrive in Thailand or anywhere else in the world.

The opportunities for prospective African migrants who might want to come to Thailand are also diminishing given the new rules regarding foreign players. Those who are already in Thailand and played in the country for a few years might be too old to secure a position in Europe. The

South–South migration of footballers is indeed a niche migration that does not leave much space for many players.

## References

Abe, Toshihiro. (2018). 'African Football Players in Cambodia,' in: *Migration and Agency in a Globalizing World: Afro-Asian Encounters*, edited by Scarlett Cornelissen & Yoichi Mine, pp. 231–245. London: Palgrave.

Akindes, Gerald A. (2013). 'South Asia and South-East Asia: New Paths of African Footballer Migration,' *Sports in Society* 14(5), pp. 684–701. https://doi.org/10.1080/14660970.2013.792486.

Bale, John & Maguire, Joseph (eds). (1994). *The Global Sports Arena: Athletic Talent Migration in an Interdependent World*. London: Frank Cass.

Bloch, Ernst. (1986). *The Principle of Hope*. Cambridge, MA: MIT Press.

Bourke, Ann. (2003). 'The Dream of Being a Professional Soccer Player: Insights on Career Development Options of Young Irish Players,' *Journal of Sport and Social Issues* 27(4), pp. 399–419. https://doi.org/10.1177/0193732503255478.

Carter, Thomas F. (2013). 'Re-Placing Sport Migrants: Moving beyond the Institutional Structures Informing International Sport Migration,' *International Review for the Sociology of Sport* 48(1), pp. 66–82. https://doi.org/10.1177/1012690211429211.

Cho, Younghan (ed). (2016). *Football in Asia: History, Culture and Business*. Oxfordshire: Routledge.

Christensen, Mette Krogh & Sørensen, Jan Kahr. (2009). 'Sport or School? Dreams and Dilemmas for Talented Young Danish Football Players,' *European Physical Education Review* 15(1), pp. 115–133.

Cleveland, Todd. (2017). *Following the Ball: The Migration of African Soccer Players Across the Portuguese Colonial Empire, 1949–1975*. Athens, OH: Ohio University Press.

Cornelissen, Scarlett & Solberg, Erik. (2007). 'Sport Mobility and Circuits of Power: The Dynamics of Football Migration in Africa and the 2010 World Cup,' *Politikon* 34(3), pp. 295–314.

Darby, Paul. (2013). 'Moving Players, Traversing Perspectives: Global Value Chains, Production Networks and Ghanaian Football Labor Migration,' *Geoforum* 50, pp. 43–53.

Darby, Paul. (2011). 'Out of Africa: The Exodus of Elite African Football Labor to Europe,' in: *Sport and Migration: Border, Boundaries and Crossings*, edited by J. Maguire & M. Falcous, pp. 245–258. Oxfordshire: Routledge.

Darby, Paul. (2010). '"Go Outside": The History, Economics and Geography of Ghanaian Football Labor Migration,' *African Historical Review* 42(1), pp. 19–41. https://doi.org/10.1080/17532523.2010.483793.

Darby, Paul. (2008). 'Ghanaian Football Labor Migration: Preliminary Observations,' Birkbeck Sport Business Center Research Paper Series. Available at: http://www.sportbusinesscentre.com/wp-content/uploads/2012/08/FeetDrain1.pdf#page=149.

Darby, Paul, Akindes, Gerard, & Kirwin, Matthew. (2007). 'Football Academies and the Migration of African Football Labor to Europe,' *Journal of Sport and Social Issues* 31(2), pp. 143–161.

De Latour, E. (2010). 'Joueurs Mondiaux, Clubs Locaux. Le Football d'Afrique en Asie,' *Politique Africaine* 118(2), pp. 63–84.

Donnelly, Peter & Petherick, Leanne. (2004). "Workers' Playtime? Child Labor at the Extremes of the Sporting Spectrum,' *Sport in Society* 7(3), pp. 301–321. https://doi.org/10.1080/1743043042000291659.

Erker, Ezra Kyrill. (2012). 'For African Footballers, the Grass is Greener in Thailand,' *Bangkok Post*, 15 April. Available at: https://www.bangkokpost.com /thailand/special-reports/288910/for-african-footballers-the-grass-is-greener-in -thailand.

Esson, James. (2015). 'Escape to Victory: Development, Youth Entrepreneurship and the Migration of Ghanaian Footballers,' *Geoforum* 64, pp. 47–55.

Esson, James. (2013). 'A Body and a Dream at a Vital Conjuncture: Ghanaian Youth, Uncertainty and the Allure of Football,' *Geoforum* 47, pp. 84–92.

Hage, Ghassan. (2003). *Against Paranoid Nationalism: Searching for Hope in a Shrinking Society*. Annandale: Pluto Press.

Kookannog, Thanadesh. (2006). *A Study of Football Teams' Management in a Competition of the Sixth Thailand Provincial Football League Division* (Master's Thesis). Thailand: Mahidol University.

Lago-Peñas, Carlos, Lago-Peñas, Santiago, & Lago, Ignacio. (2019). 'Player Migration and Soccer Performance,' *Frontiers in Psychology*. https://doi.org/10 .3389/fpsyg.2019.00616.

Luedi, Jeremy. (2018). 'Why Football Slavery is a Growing Threat to Africa's Youth,' *Asia by Africa*. Available at: https://www.asiabyafrica.com/point-a-to-a/ african-footballers-in-asia.

Magee, Johnathan & Sugden, John. (2002). 'The World at Their Feet: Professional Football and International Labor Migration,' *Journal of Sport and Social Issues* 26(4), pp. 421–437.

Murphy, Paul. (2017). *Southeast Asia: The Last Frontier of the Football World*. Available at: https://thesefootballtimes.co/2017/01/22/southeast-asia-the-last -frontier-of-the-football-world/.

Murphy, Paul. (2016). 'Why Thailand is Becoming a New Football Destination,' *The Football Times*, 26 October. Available at: https://thesefootballtimes.co/2016 /10/26/why-thailand-is-becoming-a-new-football-destination/.

Nawyn, Stephanie. (2016). 'Migration in the Global South: Exploring New Theoretical Territory,' *International Journal of Sociology* 46(2), pp. 81–84.

Panarut, Charn. (2014). 'Football, Body, Civilization and New Social Organization in the Reign of King Rama V,' in: *Thai Foot Ball: History, Power, Politics, and Masculinity*, edited by Wasan Panyagaew, Pongsakorn Sanguansak, and Jutiporn Suppanyayan, pp. 25–82. Bangkok: Center for Gambling Studies.

Poli, Raffaele. (2010). 'African Migrants in Asian and European Football: Hopes and Realities,' *Sports in Society* 13(6), pp. 1001–1011.

Siriwat, Nin & Brill, Carolina. (2015). 'Football, Migration, and Sustainability in Thailand,' *International Journal of Social Science and Humanity* 5(8), pp. 707–713.

Taylor, Matthew. (2006). 'Global Players? Football, Migration and Globalization, c. 1930–2000,' *Historical Social Research* 31(1), pp. 7–30.

Ungruhe, Christian & Esson, James. (2017). 'A Social Negotiation of Hope: Male West African Youth, Waithood and the Pursuit of Social Becoming through Football,' *Boyhood Studies* 10(1), pp. 22–43.

# 9 Looking forward

*Elżbieta M. Goździak and
Supang Chantavanich*

We hope you enjoyed reading this book based on exploratory research with and about Africans residing in Thailand. The book provides but a glimpse at the issues facing African migrants and Thai policy-makers as well as migrant advocates and migration scholars interested in this relatively new group of migrants to Thailand.

We certainly need to know more about these newcomers to Thailand. Are they immigrants or sojourners? Are they circular migrants? Is circular migration a strategy many Africans use because there are no other options? Or would Africans who established transcontinental enterprises want to continue to move freely between Africa and Thailand even if an option to reside long-term in Thailand was available? Perhaps the circular mobility suits the niche economy migrants? Are their migration patterns similar to circular migration trajectories of Chinese traders coming for business to Thailand (Chantavanich 2021)? As you have read, some Africans married local Thai women and settled. Would those with families in Africa want to settle as well and possibly bring their family members with them? Or does trans-local mobility reflect the fact that few Africans intend to settle permanently? Perhaps they want to 'settle into motion' the way post-EU accession migrants from Eastern Europe and the Baltic countries had? Is the movement between Africa and Thailand a new form of mobility? Is Zygmunt Bauman's concept of 'liquid migration' applicable here? (Bauman 1999; Engbersen 2018). These are all questions that only more robust studies can answer.

There is also much we still do not know about asylum seekers from Africa, especially Somalia and Sudan, who are brought to Thailand, a country that is not a signatory to the 1951 Refugee Convention, by human smugglers. Some of the protagonists in this volume did not know where they were going, others did not understand that they would become undocumented migrants and would have to struggle to make a living in Thailand. Were they making an informed decision to seek refuge in Thailand? Or

DOI: 10.4324/9781003286554-9

were they deceived by smugglers? The information on the smugglers is very limited. How do they operate under the radar of immigration authorities? Are they part of an organized international smuggling network? Or are they opportunists operating on their own? Are Thai citizens involved in smuggling operations?

The research that informs this volume focused mainly on African migrants and *their* perceptions of discrimination, othering, and racism. Where do these attitudes stem from? Do they mirror attitudes towards Africans in other parts of Asia? There is no evidence of violent clashes between African migrants and Thai citizens. Certainly nothing similar to the situation in South Asia or China. In the last few years, there has been a steady increase in the assaults against Africans in South Asia. 'Racial discrimination along with deep-seated prejudices play a major role in such mob violence, often entangled with stereotypical accusations of kidnapping, drug peddling, pimping and even cannibalism' (Kooria 2020: 353). In 2020, international media reported extensively on evictions and forced detention of Africans living in China, especially in the southern city of Guangzhou (Marsh et al. 2020). Unfortunately, these recent examples of racial discrimination are not new. As Winslow Robertson (2020) writes, there is a long history of violence and discrimination against Africans in China, including the 1988–89 Nanjing racial turmoil (Sautman 1994) and the 2014 Ebola outbreak in West Africa resulting in forced quarantine of Africans living in China, to name a few examples.

According to Robertson (2020), Chinese perceptions of Africans draw from two separate narratives: that Africans are dangerous, disease-carrying individuals, and also a tolerated minority subject to the whims of state violence. The Thai police certainly think that most Africans in Thailand are dangerous criminals and Thai immigration authorities consider them illegal migrants. Even asylum seekers registered with the United Nations High Commissioner for Refugees (UNHCR) are at the mercy of Thai authorities who do not always accord them the necessary protection.

But what about members of the general public? In order to fully understand attitudes towards Africans, we must also study members of the wider Thai society. The perceptions as expressed by African migrants themselves offer but one side of the story. We must understand better the origins of the construction of blackness in contemporary Thailand. Writing about Africans in China, Shanshan Lan (2017) argues that there is 'no overarching or homogenized discourse of anti-black racism in China, due to the heterogeneity of both the Chinese and African communities and the existence of the Chinese and white gazes in defining blackness as a racialized identity' (Lan 2017: 191). According to Lan, the Chinese knowledge of Black people is drawn from several sources; 'traditional Chinese esthetic values which favor light skin over dark skin; racialized images of blacks in Western literature and media; Chinese state propaganda such as the Sino-African friendship discourse; Chinese language media; personal experience, and hearsay' (Lan 2017: 190).

There are many similarities in Thailand. Thai preference for light skin is evident in the cosmetic industry that promotes *peau khao* (white skin) and fashions a racist social technology (Persaud 2005). The idea that black is ugly and white is beautiful seems to stem from the notion that darker skin represents a life of manual labor in the sun and therefore a lower social class with a lack of money and education, and white skin is a sign of privilege.

Like China, Thailand opened a new diplomatic chapter focusing on Africa. In 2013, the Thai–Africa Initiative was launched to increase engagement beyond the country's immediate neighborhood in the ASEAN region. By 2017, Thailand elevated this initiative into a new policy of Thai–Africa Partnership for Sustainable Development (Tarrosy 2018). The media propagates an ignorant stereotype of white desirability, often mocking the dark skinned (whether they're Thais from Isaan, southern Muslim citizens, or neighboring Cambodians) in failed and tone-deaf humor which feeds the natural racism, discrimination, and bigotry (Rojanaphruk 2020).

Unlike in China, few Thai people have had any meaningful relationships with Africans and their opinions about Black people are usually formed on the basis of hearsay or distorted portrayals of mixed-race protagonists of Thai soap operas. Writing about African traders in Guangzhou, Lan emphasizes the fact that the convergence of internal and international migration in South China

> enabled a different style of racial learning, which is not based primarily on secondary sources or Western influence, but on personal interaction in grass roots trade activities. Due to the concentration of Sino-African trade activities in the informal economy, many Chinese who come into daily contact with Africans are from non-elite backgrounds, the majority being migrant workers and petty.
>
> (Lan 2017: 193)

The gems traders in Chanthaburi certainly have frequent and meaningful contacts with African gems traders as they engage in mutually beneficial business. A few gems traders married local Thai women. However, members of the wider Chanthaburi community do not see the benefits the African traders bring to their town. They see Africans as the undesirable Others (Vungsiriphisal, this volume).

Some writers believe that things are changing and younger, more cosmo-politan Thais have much more positive attitudes towards mixed-race actors and entertainers. Thai–Mali vlogger Natthawadee 'Suzie' Waikalo has been gaining media coverage and TikTok followers among Thais since the Black Lives Matter protests in the US (Thaitrakulpanich 2020b). Rusameekae Fagerlund, a gay TV talk show host and actor, who has Senegalese, Thai, and American ancestry has also gained many fans among young Thais (Thaitrakulpanich 2020a). To what extent the support on social media will extend to real life remains to be seen. Natthawadee Waikalo was fired from her job, because her physical characteristics and demeanor allegedly made the company look bad.

These attitudes do not bode well for integration, but we do not know much about integration, economic or socio-cultural, of Africans residing in Thailand. While there is extensive research on migrant workers' integration into the Thai economy, these studies cover mainly Asian migrant workers working in Thailand under various bilateral agreements (OECD 2017). Our exploratory research suggests that while Somalis, Nigerians, and others sur-vive in Thailand, they seem to operate in the niche economy, live in ethnic enclaves, and are not part of the Thai social fabric.

We could go on listing topics that need migration scholars' attention, but even the most comprehensive list of research topics is not enough. Attention needs to be also drawn to methodologies that would ensure high-quality research benefiting all concerned. If the African diaspora is to benefit from the research, members of the local African communities need to be involved in different types of community-based participatory research. Participatory research needs to highlight the methodological shift from research carried out 'on' migrants to research carried out 'with' migrants, and most recently, research carried out 'by' migrants (e.g., Bertozzi 2010; Zlotnick 2020). Three contributors to this volume are Africans themselves, but only one is an immigrant who has lived and worked in Thailand for 17 years. He definitely brings the insider's perspective to his research. The other African authors used their common ancestry to access the African diaspora in Bangkok, but their privileged position as graduate students, residing temporarily in Thailand, did not position them as true insiders.

Contributors to this volume have been partial to qualitative research using small snowball samples. All of this research was conducted in one place, often a small neighborhood. Future studies ought to consider multi-sited ethnography, a method of data collection that allows to follow a topic or social problem through different field sites and analytically explore transnational processes, people in motion, and ideas that extend over mul-tiple locations (Marcus 1995). Contemporary migration scholarship is increasingly focusing on the analysis of the effects of migration on sending communities. It would be very useful to study families and communities left behind and explore not merely the effects of financial remittances but also socio-cultural remittances (Goździak & Main 2020; Levitt & Lamba-Nieves 2013).

While the African community in Thailand is still very small, the statistical information on African migrants, including the diversity of African communities, is very limited. The Thai Census Bureau does not collect data similar to the information included in the American Community Survey (ACS), the premier source for detailed population and housing information about US residents. The ACS provides detailed analysis of the foreign-born population in the United States, including data on nativity, length of time in the country, educational attainment, homeownership, facility in heritage language/s and English, and many others. This data helps local officials, community leaders, and businesses to understand the changes taking place in their communities. The Thai Census might want to emulate data gathering strategies deployed by other immigration countries. Singapore, for example, includes the foreign-born in its population survey, including data on immigration status citizenship, permanent residency, and mixed marriages between native Singaporeans and the foreign-born. The government indicates that 'Immigration helps to moderate the impact of ageing and low birth rates in our citizen (SC) population, and keeps it from shrinking over the longer term. The pace of immigration will continue to be kept measured and stable' (Population in Brief 2021: 17). Collecting data on immigrants helps Singapore plan for the future. In Thailand, some predict that more West Africans will arrive in the country to seek better opportunities. West Africans already constitute the largest group of African visitors in ASEAN. More information on Africans interested in coming to Thailand would help policy-makers understand this group of potential newcomers and plan better for their arrival.

Research and data are essential, but they mean very little if not accompanied by actions. Who needs to spring to action? The simple answer is everybody: members of the African diaspora, Thai policy-makers, law enforcement, local community members, migrant advocates, and journalists, to give just a few examples. While rights-based immigration and integration policies at the national level are important, action at the community level where the web of local relationships determine the immigrant experience, is equally if not more valuable.

Our exploratory research suggests that the news media reinforce stereotypes about Africans and significantly affect how the Thai public views migrants from the African continent. Unfortunately, media coverage of African migrants frequently focuses on the criminal activities without emphasizing that not all Africans residing in Thailand have committed crimes; the vast majority are upstanding members of the society. Thai law enforcement has a role to play in correcting these misperceptions promulgated by the media. When migrants are portrayed as 'criminals' and 'illegals,' conflicts ensue.

Integration depends on the empowerment of immigrants for participation in the wider community, both economically and socially. It is important to stress opportunities and obligations as well as rights. There is an important role that mediating institutions such as local governments, schools, trade associations, and civic organizations can play in facilitating immigrant integration. They can provide opportunities for Thai people and Africans to meet in person and discuss both differences and similarities. For example, a conversation about emigration might bring to light the fact that many Thai people also migrate. Over 200,000 people self-reported as Thai in the 2010 US Census, a nearly 60% increase from the previous decade. Los Angeles has the largest concentration of Thais outside of Thailand, with local organizations estimating up to 80,000 Thais living in LA County (Thepboriruk 2015). Given the recent worldwide anti-Asian sentiments, Thais and Africans might benefit from conversations about discrimination and racism.

The research community, policy-makers, and migration activists have to come together to spearhead these conversations and make sure that they are not happening in an empirical vacuum.

## References

Bauman, Zygmunt. (1999). *Liquid Modernity*. Oxford: Polity Press.

Bertozzi, Rita. (2010). 'A Participatory Approach to Research with Migrant Working Adolescents,' *Migration Letters* 7(1), pp. 57–67.

Chantavanich, Supang. (2021). 'China's Rising Influence in Thailand: Translocal Human Mobility and Its Impact,' in: *China's Rise in Mainland ASEAN: Regional Evidence and Local Responses*, edited by Suthiphand Chirathivat, Buddhagarn Rutchatorn, and Wasutadorn Nakawiroj, pp. 133–154. Singapore: World Scientific.

Engbersen, Godfried. (2018). 'Liquid Migration and Its Consequences for Local Integration Policies,' in: *Between Mobility and Migration: The Multi-Level Governance of Intra-European Movement*, edited by Peter Scholten, and Mark van Ostaijen, pp. 63–76. Cham: Springer.

Goździak, Elzbieta M., and Main, Izabella. (2020). 'Transnational Mobility and Socio-Cultural Remittances: The Case of Polish Women in Norway and Poland,' *Ethnologia Europaea* 50(1). https://doi.org/10.16995/ee.1207.

Kooria, Mahmood. (2020). 'Introduction: Narrating Africa in South Asia,' *South Asian History and Culture* 4(4), pp. 351–362. https://doi.org/10.1080/19472498.2020.1827592.

Lan, Shanshan. (2017). *Mapping the New African Diaspora in China: Race and the Cultural Politics of Belonging.* London: Routledge.

Levitt, Peggy, and Lamba-Nieves, Deepak. (2013). 'Rethinking Social Remittances and the Migration-Development Nexus from the Perspective of Time,' *Migration Letters* 10(1), pp. 11–22. https://doi.org/10.33182/ml.v10i1.107

Marcus, George E. (1995). 'Ethnography In/of the World System: The Emergence of Multi-sited Ethnography,' *Annual Review of Anthropology* 24(1), pp. 95–117.

Marsh, Jenni, Deng, Shawn, and Gan, Nectar. (2020). 'Africans in Guangzhou Are on Edge, after Many Are Left Homeless amid Rising Xenophobia as China Fights a Second Wave of Coronavirus,' *CNN*. Available at: https://www.cnn.com/2020/04/10/china/africans-guangzhou-china-coronavirus-hnk-intl/index.html.

OECD/ILO. (2017). *How Immigrants Contribute to Thailand's Economy.* Paris: OECD Publishing. https://doi.org/10.1787/9789264287747-en.

Persaud, Walter H. (2005). 'Gender, Race and Global Modernity: A Perspective from Thailand,' *Globalizations* 2(2), pp. 210–227. https://doi.org/10.1080/14747730500202214.

Robertson, Winslow. (2020). 'A Brief History of Anti-black Violence in China,' Available at: https://africasacountry.com/2020/05/a-brief-history-of-anti-black-violence-in-china.

Rojanaphruk, Pravit. (2020). 'Opinion: From American Racism to Thai Chauvinism,' *Khaosod News*, 7 June. Available at: https://www.khaosodenglish.com/opinion/2020/06/07/opinion-from-american-racism-to-thai-chauvinism/.

Sautman, Barry. (1994). 'Anti-black Racism in Post-Mao China,' *The China Quarterly* 138, pp. 413–437. https://doi.org/10.1017/S0305741000035827.

Singapore Department of Statistics. (2021). 'Population in Brief 2021,' Available at: https://www.population.gov.sg/files/media-centre/publications/Population-in-brief-2021.pdf.

Thaitrakulpanich, Asaree. (2020a). 'Meet Rusameekae, Thailand's Half-Black LGBT Star,' *Khao Sod English*, 6 August. Available at: https://www.khaosodenglish.com/life/arts/2020/08/06/meet-rusameekae-thailands-half-black-lgbt-star/.

Tarrosy, Istvan. (2018). 'Thailand's Engagement with Africa: Yet another 'unusual suspect' is Intensifying Relations with African Countries. How Far Can It Go?,' *The Diplomat*, 28 February. Available at: https://thediplomat.com/2018/03/thailands-engagement-with-africa/.

Thaitrakulpanich, Asaree. (2020b). 'What It's Like to Be Half-Black, Half-Thai: Suzie's Story,' *Khao Sod English*, 12 June. Available at https://www.khaosodenglish.com/culture/net/2020/06/12/what-its-like-to-be-half-black-half-thai-suzies-story/.

Thepboriruk, Kanjana. (2015). *Thai in Diaspora: Language and Identity in Los Angeles, California*, Doctoral dissertation. University of Hawaii at Manoa. http://hdl.handle.net/10125/51132.

Zlotnick, Cheryl. (2020). 'Migrant Studies Using the Community-Based Participatory Research Partnership Approach,' *European Journal of Public Health* 30(5). https://doi.org/10.1093/eurpub/ckaa166.731.

# Index

For Product Safety Concerns and Information please contact our EU
representative GPSR@taylorandfrancis.com Taylor & Francis Verlag GmbH,
Kaufingerstraße 24, 80331 München, Germany


Printed and bound by CPI Group (UK) Ltd, Croydon, CR0 4YY
11/04/2025
01844012-0009